# From Pitiful to *Beautiful*

## Intimacy with The Lord

*"I felt Him close to me. I was surrounded by His warmth."*

Becky Keener

From Pitiful to Beautiful
Intimacy with The Lord.

Copyright © 2021 Becky Keener.

All rights reserved. This book is protected by the copyright laws of the United States of America. This book may not be copied or printed for commercial gain or profit.

Unless otherwise identified, Scripture quotations are from the Holy Bible, New Kings James Version Copyright © 1982 Thomas Nelson, Inc. Used by permission. All rights reserved.

Emphasis within Scripture quotations is the author's own. Italics in Scripture are for emphasis.

ISBN: 9798757256269

## DEDICATION

I dedicate this book to my children, Casey and BreAnn. The love I have for you caused me to pursue Jesus and discover that He is real and near. I wanted to be a better person, not only for myself, but for you too. I pray you live in the depths of God's love all the days of your life. It's my desire that you will pursue Jesus as I did and discover that He is real and near. I love you both with my whole heart.

# CONTENTS

Forward viii

Introduction x

**Section 1:**

## *Intimacy*

Chapter 1   Intimacy is a Must   1

Chapter 2   The Beauty of the Night   4

Chapter 3   His Breath   6

## *Humility*

Chapter 4   Come to Me   8

Chapter 5   Essence of Humility   10

## *Revelation of Christ*

Chapter 6   Faith of a Champion   13

Chapter 7   My Beloved   16

Chapter 8   The Dedication   18

Chapter 9   The Lion and The Lamb   20

**Section 2:**

## *Rejection*

| | | |
|---|---|---|
| Chapter 10 | Wanted | 24 |
| Chapter 11 | Walked Blessed | 27 |
| Chapter 12 | Desire of All Nations | 30 |

## *Betrayal*

| | | |
|---|---|---|
| Chapter 13 | Rise Above it | 33 |
| Chapter 14 | Walk Softly | 36 |

## *Self-Pity*

| | | |
|---|---|---|
| Chapter 15 | He Sees All | 39 |
| Chapter 16 | For Your Good | 43 |
| Chapter 17 | On Things Above | 46 |

## *Guilt*

| | | |
|---|---|---|
| Chapter 18 | You Know My Heart | 49 |
| Chapter 19 | Justice Served | 52 |
| Chapter 20 | Covenant Keeper | 55 |
| Chapter 21 | Believing Him | 58 |

| Chapter 22 | Heaven's Angels | 62 |

## *Fear*

| Chapter 23 | Spirit Lead Me | 65 |
| Chapter 24 | He Knows Me | 68 |
| Chapter 25 | The River | 71 |

**Section 3:**

## *Love*

| Chapter 26 | Maturity is Power | 75 |
| Chapter 27 | The Dance | 78 |
| Chapter 28 | God is Love | 82 |
| Chapter 29 | Belonging | 85 |

## *Peace*

| Chapter 30 | Comforter | 88 |
| Chapter 31 | Finding Treasure | 91 |

## *Joy*

| Chapter 32 | Pursue Joy | 94 |
| Chapter 33 | Listen to the Rain | 97 |

## *Compassion*

| | | |
|---|---|---|
| Chapter 34 | Flickering Stars | 100 |
| Chapter 35 | Warring Soldiers | 102 |
| Chapter 36 | Butterflies | 106 |

**Section 4:**

## *Repentance*

| | | |
|---|---|---|
| Chapter 37 | Forgiven | 109 |
| Chapter 38 | God is Good | 111 |
| Chapter 39 | Blessed Beyond the Curse | 114 |
| Chapter 40 | Embrace the call | 117 |

**Section 5:**

## *Searching*

| | | |
|---|---|---|
| Chapter 41 | His Strength | 121 |
| Chapter 42 | Heart Be Still | 123 |
| Chapter 43 | Deeper Still | 125 |
| Chapter 44 | Gold Digger | 127 |

# Forward

Following Jesus is more than an intellectual belief. Jesus is real. He is a Person. To follow Jesus is to pursue an active relationship with Him, as a Person. When Jesus called his first disciples, it was to "be with Him." (Mark 3:14-15) He still desires for people to be with Him.

In more than 30 years of church leadership, I have discovered that in today's modern Christianity, it is popular in the church to *talk* about a relationship with God, while few ever *experience* that relationship with Him.

I met Becky while we were establishing a state-wide network of prayer in West Virginia. Of all the people and prayer leaders we met during this process, Becky was the most inquisitive. You could sense that she valued prayer and desired to understand something thoroughly before getting involved with it. What quickly became evident was her desire and passion to truly know and experience God in a real and personal way.

Through this book, Becky takes the reader on a journey as she interacts with God as a real Person. Conversations are shared, direction is revealed, and insights are given as she talks about her personal interactions with God.

While it can be interesting to read about someone else's experiences, you can experience God for yourself. Becky desires that her experiences will inspire you to be sensitive to the voice of God in your own life and that you too can "be with Him."

So read and be challenged to grow deeper in your pursuit to *know* Jesus!


Pastor Jay Morgan
Founder, *Appalachia Prayer Center Ministries*
Author, *Discover Discipleship*

# Introduction

I believe The Lord spoke to my heart and asked me to share my healing journey to help others heal from anxiety, depression, and panic attacks. It has been a genuine desire of my heart to see people healed and set free in Christ. As I share my journey with you, you will read some of my personal experiences with The Lord. I pray they speak to you. I've asked The Lord to grip your heart, giving you all you need to be made whole again.

I'll share how intimacy with The Lord opened the door for me to become a brand-new person, someone I could live with. Through intimacy, I fell in love with Jesus at a whole new level. I want to share His love so that you will fall deeper in love with Him just as I did.

Common snares of the enemy such as fear, guilt, and rejection kept me bound and separated me from God. Though these were some of my darkest days, they became some of my most beautiful. The Lord helped me, and I believe He will help you, too! You may not have emotional and mental struggles, but you may know someone who does. I pray this book will encourage you.

As I traveled this healing journey, I prayed that I would be healed one day. Little by little, layer by layer, Jesus peeled away those things that were not healthy and were not of Him. He would gently deal with an issue and graciously heal my heart piece by piece.

Yes, I am a work in progress and will be for the rest of my life. I've come too far to turn back now. I fall in love with Jesus over and over again. My longing will never end because Jesus captured my heart. He has ravished my heart and I am His.

Today I am nowhere near where I once was, in that awful state of "pitiful." Instead, I hear Him call me "beautiful!" My one desire for you is that not only will you enjoy and learn from the "From *Pitiful to Beautiful, Intimacy with The Lord"* devotional, but that you would receive all that I received and more. Read a chapter or two every day during your quiet time with The Lord. Take a moment and listen to Him. I believe He will speak to you. Take notes, keep a journal, and commit to your healing.

May God reveal Himself to you, heal you, and bring you into wholeness. God Bless you!

## From Pitiful to Beautiful-Intimacy is a Must!

Depression, anxiety, panic attacks, and mental torment once ruled my life. I was born again and went to church faithfully but still had a serious problem. I needed healing! My church family was (and even to this day) has been incredible. Pastors and close friends prayed for me and always encouraged me with words of hope. I believe keeping "good company" contributed a lot toward my healing, but I needed more.

I had no understanding about *"intimacy with The Lord."* I heard about it and soon discovered I needed it. Nothing I tried *cured* me or gave me a sense of peace. My doctor prescribed medication and I followed his instructions, yet, all the while seeking God to help me. I didn't want to be dependent on medicine, and in my experience, they didn't help me the way I needed them to. For others, medication may work, but that wasn't the case for me. The medication took the edge off, but my mind and emotions were racing terribly. I *needed* healing from The Lord!

I quoted scriptures and voiced an abundance of praise. Yet, the panic did not stop! I did not know why. God's Word is powerful, and He loves our praise. So, what was the problem? Something wasn't right. I wasn't sure what else to *do,* so I decided just to *be*.

I began seeking God in the quiet of the night. After my family would go to sleep, I would go to my front porch and spend my nights seeking Jesus. I searched for God. I started in the fall and continued seeking God throughout the winter months every single night. I was desperate to find Him and discover if He were real. I needed to know if The Lord would help me. I had made up my mind, if He was real, He could help me. Did He want to heal me? I wasn't sure, but I was longing for answers and adamantly seeking Him! I had to try.

By reading God's Word, I knew that King David had more than just a few problems, so I decided to begin reading in Psalms. I just read the Bible out loud to God. This was the only way I felt close to Him.

I soon discovered that intimacy with God was a heart-to-heart relationship and a must. It was a spirit-to-spirit bond that I needed to truly live.

Believing I was on the right path and that I would discover the realness of God, I kept seeking and reading night after night. Once I got to Psalm 121, things began to happen.

***Seek The Lord while He may be found, Call upon Him while He is near." Isaiah 55:6.*** *If you have not developed intimacy with God, or need to discover more, now is a perfect time. He does not disappoint.*

**From Pitiful to Beautiful-The Beauty of the Night**

I will never forget these words, **"I will lift my eyes to the hills, from whence comes my help? My help comes from the Lord who made the heavens and the earth." Psalms 121:1-2.** I was desperately searching for The Lord in the night, and I found Him. When I look back now, it was the place He drew me to meet with Him heart-to-heart and spirit-to-spirit.

I remember looking up at the stars in the sky with tears running down my face saying, "You made this, you made me!" A true and living God encountered my heart in the cold night's air during the darkest hours of my life. I thought I knew God, but in reality, I had just begun to feel Him near me. I stepped through a spiritual door of intimacy that changed my life forever!

I finally experienced Him as real and near.

His Spirit approached me, gently persuading me to open my heart to Him. My Master Creator knew every part of me, even my inward parts. I could feel Him looking through me. In that moment, I melted. "He's here; He's real." I then realized that it was "inner" healing that I needed. I knew the "inner" was required for Him to heal me.

Jesus wanted to gently touch and mend every broken part of my heart. It was the scariest thing I have ever been asked to do. It was hard to lay my heart bare and broken before anyone, even God. He wanted all of me. He wanted every secret, every thought, and every emotion. All that I had He wanted. Little by little, I did it.

To surrender to the Creator of the Universe was far greater than I could have ever imagined. I had to admit that I could not fix myself. I had to humble myself and surrender to Him! I was terrified, but I took a giant leap of faith into my Creator's hands. I have never regretted my decision. Honestly, every night with Him is Beautiful!

*I want to encourage you to take that leap of faith into the hands of a loving God. You can lay your heart bare. He is waiting for you.*

**From Pitiful to Beautiful-His Breath!**

When the Bible says "knowledge" of God, it means to *know* Him heart-to-heart and spirit-to-spirit. That's what I needed; I needed to know Him intimately. My emotions were my biggest problem. I needed to *feel* love, peace, joy, and a connection to someone greater (God) than myself. Our emotions can tear us apart, but *His* emotions will mend us. For me, it all started with a kiss.

I continued spending nights on my front porch with The Lord. It was there that I learned I needed a revelation of The Word of God. I needed to experience the scriptures, not just quote them. I believed there had to be a way to step into them spiritually and *feel* their power. I needed a deeper, a more in depth, encounter. I *had* to have the presence of The Lord; *head* knowledge didn't take me far. It's been *heart* knowledge that's healed me, and it is *heart* knowledge I continue to seek.

**"Kiss me with the kisses of your mouth." Song of Solomon 1:2b.** To simplify, the kiss means, "Breathe your breath in me, from your spirit to my spirit." When I think of this scripture, I still get chills! I never dreamed I would experience Him in the way I did. I never thought this scripture would come alive in me. To become intimate in the purest sense with the God of all creation was far beyond what I could grasp, but it wasn't too far for Him.

One night, during an ice storm, I was on my front porch, and I was freezing, yet I was basking in The Lord's presence. I felt Him close to me. I was surrounded by His warmth. His presence overshadowed me with peace. He was there! Love was filling my heart. It was the most beautiful feeling in the world. He was speaking secrets to my heart and touching my emotions deep within me. I didn't want this encounter to end. I said, "Lord, I am so cold, but I don't want to leave this moment." I was desperate for Him. Immediately, He gently blew warm air over me, keeping me warm and in our moment. My feet instantly warmed up and my heart melted. His Word came alive, and I experienced His kiss!

*May The Lord's love for you be revealed to your heart. Meet with Him and bask in His presence. Invite Him to kiss you with the kisses of His mouth.*

## From Pitiful to Beautiful-Come to Me

I could feel the weight of depression so strong; it was almost unbearable, making it difficult to function. My days were hard. They were heavy. I was going through the "motions" of life, but I was not enjoying it.

One morning while in a prayer meeting, I was experiencing high anxiety. I could hardly sit still. After the meeting, I asked for prayer. Even after prayer, I still had anxiety. "When will this ever end?" I thought. I set my heart to wait on The Lord. I was not leaving until I got answers. I waited, prayed, and waited again.

That's when I heard The Lord say, "You must come to me as a little child." While He was speaking these words, I suddenly felt like a little girl again. I could feel the innocence and I could even feel my hair messed up and in my face. It's hard to describe, but it was genuine, authentic, and real.

I needed to remember how it felt to be a child again. As The Lord lingered with me, I felt my heart shift toward Him in humility. In that moment, I felt God's peace. The Lord explained the importance of humility to me. We can't be saved without first humbling ourselves and admitting we are sinners needing a Savior. Unfortunately, that was as far as I went. I had a small level of humility but a large level of pride, which was hard to swallow.

I had to go down. I knew God was real and near, but there was more. If I could not save myself, why would I think I could heal myself? I had to yield and allow Him to do His work in me. It was hard to do, but I knew it was something I had to do, because there was no other way. As I took baby steps in surrender to Him, I was opening my heart for God to heal me. Opening my heart to Him was the key to unlocking the beginning of healing inside of me.

***Assuredly, I say to you, unless you are converted, and become as little children, you will by no means enter into the Kingdom of Heaven. Matthew 18:3.*** *There's no anxiety or depression in His Kingdom. Enter in and be healed!*

**From Pitiful to Beautiful-Essence of Humility**

The one thing I learned about pride is that it's not always arrogance. Pride includes self-protection, self-preservation, and self-centeredness. We can be kind and soft-spoken and all the while be polluted with pride. Selfish motives are not always easily detected. Quiet does not mean humble. God knows the difference!

One night I had a dream. I was hiding behind a door and as I opened it, I heard someone say, "Becky, The Lord wants to see you." I stepped out to find a cinder block wall as high as I could see. I knew The Lord was behind that wall, and I knew the wall was mine, not His. It was apparent to me that a lot of walls needed to come down. We must humble ourselves and let our guard down, even when it is hard to do.

Satan is an enemy that tries to stop us from opening up to God. He convinces us that when we open our hearts to God, we open up to him, too, but this is a lie! It is a lie that causes us to self-protect and build walls. Just remember, we are asked to open up our hearts to God only, *not* Satan. When we open up our hearts to God, it is safe.

Pride threw the devil down, but humility raised Jesus up. The Bible says in **Philippians 2:8-9, "And being found in appearance as a man, He humbled Himself and became obedient to the point of death, even death of the cross. Therefore God highly exalted Him and gave Him the name which is above every name."** According to the scriptures, Jesus is the very *Essence of Humility*.

Jesus taught us to pick up our cross and follow Him, or we are not His disciples. Taking up our cross includes humbling ourselves, letting our walls down, and opening our hearts to God. When we walk in humility, we walk the path of God. When we are high in pride, we walk the road of the enemy. We will encounter God as we choose humility. If we choose pride, the enemy comes with it.

My perspective was not based in truth, but in lies and hurts, which affected my emotions. I built these walls. I had many mixed feelings, but most of the time what I felt was anxiety. I am not implying someone with anxiety has all the negative emotions that I did. You may have few or you may have none. That would be for you and The Lord to discover together. I only want to say, "Be blessed and enjoy the journey!"

*I pray the very essence of humility encounters you and fills you completely, leaving you healed and whole in Jesus name.*

**From Pitiful to Beautiful-The Faith of a Champion**

Late one evening, I was soaking in God's presence and gazing at the cross with my spiritual eyes. I kept seeing the Lord's thighs. I would scan over His entire body, yet my eyes would return to His thighs, Holy Spirit was revealing Christ to me. These thighs were not skinny or puny, long or lanky. No. No. No. They were large and muscular. They were dirty and bloody. I was shocked! I never thought of Jesus as a masculine warrior, but that is definitely who *He* is! It nearly took my breath away to see such fierce strength.

The Holy Spirit spoke scripture to me. He was declaring, **"My Beloved, His legs are pillars of marble set on bases of fine gold. His countenance is like Lebanon, Excellent as the cedars." Song of Solomon 5:15**. In that moment, I understood that Jesus *is* strong and powerful, and

He would always be the Victor!

I continued to watch the Lord carry His cross. He carried it with great strength and purpose. Though His legs wobbled from pure exhaustion, His heart was set: He would not and could not fail. He kept going.

The endurance of our Lord is indescribable. Determined to make it to that hill for His bride, He would die for her. He would resurrect for her. There was no stopping Him. He was set! Oh, how my heart grew more in love with Him!

What great faith! Jesus was beaten, torn, and tired, yet, determined and strong. He is always faithful to His cause. He is mightier than cancer! He is mightier than diabetes! He is mightier than mental illness! He is mightier than drug addiction! He is mightier than death! Jesus destroyed all the power of panic disorders the day that He carried them to the cross with *all* the strength and determination that was in Him. For the joy that was set before Him, He endured the cross. **(Hebrews 12:2)**

The most extraordinary faith I believe we can ever see is the faith of Jesus. For the sake of love, Jesus refused to fail, love is why He endured. Now, we must lean into Him and let Him lead our way. We can trust Him no matter the outcome, for He is faithful and strong.

*Seek Him. He will amaze you! Jesus is the Champion and our Victor! He will not fail you!*

**From Pitiful to Beautiful-My Beloved**

Though it may be impossible to see or experience all of whom God is, I have had some incredible insights I would like to share with you that brought me so much joy. I pray that you would behold His beauty and fall deeper in love with our King. May the Spirit of wisdom and revelation come to you, unlocking the knowledge of Christ within your heart!

The Lord gave me the most beautiful dream several years ago that I will never forget. It was while I was battling panic attacks and depression. Holy Spirit woke me up several times that night, and each time I woke, He impressed upon me to pray in a way that I had never prayed before. "Sevenfold Spirit of God, come and minister to me." I wrestled back and forth in prayer and finally fell asleep.

In this dream, I was in the town where my grandparents lived. There was a bridge over a river and a crowd of people on the other side. As I crossed the bridge to stand in the crowd, I saw two men making their way through. The crowd split and immediately knew which man was Jesus! No one there doubted it either. Everyone knew who He was! **Song of Solomon 5:10 "My beloved is white and ruddy, chief among ten thousand."**

He was incredible and breathtaking! I don't believe I have ever seen such excellence and majesty in all my life. There is nothing to compare to Him. There is such awe around Him that it's almost unbelievable. It wasn't just His appearance that captured me; it was His presence! He drew me to Him. It was the way He made me feel when I was around Him- wanted, important, and celebrated. I remember His majestic presence more clearly than I remember His appearance. My legs still tremble thinking about Him.

*May excitement arise in you as you pursue to know your Beloved!*

**From Pitiful to Beautiful-The Dedication**

I want to continue with the dream The Lord gave me. As I looked closer at Jesus, I saw a black curl lying on His shoulder. **Song of Solomon 5:11: "His head is like finest gold, His locks are wavy and black as a raven**." As I looked closer at that black curl, a revelation about Jesus came to me.

Jesus came to earth entirely dedicated to God's plan, willingly taking up His Cross and redeeming His bride. He was ripped apart so we can be mended and made whole. Oh, how we are loved! Every sin we've ever committed, every sin ever committed against us, every sickness, every disease, every lie, and every delusion from hell, Christ willingly took upon Himself. He was crucified, and through His blood, He brought healing for us. He was not *made* to give up His life, but He *willingly* gave it. That is dedication. That is commitment. Wow, think about it, this should give you goose bumps!

I needed to know this kind of love as I struggled with anxiety and depression. I needed to know that God was faithful and strong and that I could depend on Him. It was hard for me to overcome fear and trust Him. I never recognized God's love or His faithfulness to me. Now I realize that He is committed to me, and He is committed to everyone that belongs to Him. His strength is undeniable.

      I believe it is necessary to know the depth of God's love so we can grow in it and obtain the peace and joy He died to give us. For me, it was essential that I felt that love. I needed my faith increased in believing God loved me. If I can't feel His love or experience it, then how can I recognize it, know it, and embrace it? I needed to feel something. I needed to experience something real. God knew my need and didn't leave me helpless. He came and gave me just what I needed. He's that dedicated.

*As you seek Him, I pray you will see Him in all His beauty and glory. He is wholeheartedly committed to you. Feel it. Experience it. Know it. Embrace it.*

## From Pitiful to Beautiful-The Lion and the Lamb

In the final part of my dream, I noticed that the Lord's shoulders were not narrow, and not weak. He was broad, muscular, and powerful. He was bad! I mean bad to the bone! "**His hands are rods of gold set with beryl. His body is carved ivory inlaid with sapphires. Song of Solomon 5:14**. He was fierce; He was beautiful, powerful, and breathtaking. I knew no one could ever beat Him.

I knew that He was a warring King and had just come back from winning a war fought for the one He loved, *His bride*. He had devoured all her enemies. This conquering, victorious King was the fiercest and most ferocious thing I had ever seen. Who would dare rouse Him? I understand when the Bible says that even the demons tremble when they hear His name. Jesus. He is undoubtedly the All-Mighty, All-Powerful One.

I saw that, in a split second, He could tear His bride's enemies to shreds. They were no match for Him. On the other end of that split second, He could compassionately and tenderly hold her shaking little hand, keeping her safe. He loved her so much that He fought for her every need. Wow! The way He loves us! It took me a while, but I now realize this was just a small glimpse of both the Lion and the Lamb, the warrior King, and the gentle Lover. He is a tender Lamb toward the bride that He loves, but He is as fierce as a hungry Lion toward her enemies.

As the dream continued, the Lord took me to another place. He turned and pointed to the sky behind us and asked, "Can you see?" In the background, I could hear these words being softly chanted "signs, wonders, signs, wonders." As I looked, I saw small blue stars flickering in the sky.

The Lord began to show me objects that made little sense to me. I particularly remember a yellow and purple light around some of the objects, and I couldn't understand where the light was coming from. I noticed that nothing was plugged into a power outlet. I was stumped. The Lord patiently explained, in detail, what each object was, what they meant, and how they functioned. I nodded my head in agreement, but I couldn't understand it. Yet, The Lord did not get frustrated with me. He was tender and patient. He never made me feel dumb or inadequate. He was gentle.

*May visitations and encounters with the eternal realm flood your souls with God's Glory. Pray and ask The Lord to reveal Himself to you. He is amazing!*

*Prayers~ Thoughts~ Impressions*

**From Pitiful to Beautiful-Wanted**

There was a time in my life that I walked in a constant mode of rejection. It was rooted deep in my heart. Rejection influenced my everyday life, negatively, of course. I don't know how it got there, but I remember when God shined His light on it and drove the rejection out!

I came home from church one night feeling hurt and unwanted. That's how rejection feels. No one said anything to offend me, but I had this pain of rejection in my heart. My thoughts were going wild. I had thoughts like "they don't really want me around" and "because I am a woman," and "no one likes me." These thoughts had my emotions in a total uproar.

That night I went to bed crying. I couldn't seem to stop. I sobbed for a while. As I continued crying, I could tell something was happening. I felt relief. I could feel the pain leaving my heart. So, I asked The Lord, "What was that?" He spoke to me and said, "It was rejection."

I didn't know I had rejection issues. I hadn't heard of that before. "Inner Healing" and "Emotional Wellness" were all new to me. I peacefully fell asleep that night and awoke the next morning feeling brand new and refreshed! I noticed as time went on, my thinking had changed. Words like "unwanted" and "they don't like me" left my thinking. I don't know if negative emotions led to the bad thoughts or if the bad thoughts led to negative emotions. Either way, God changed both drastically. I am so thankful.

The Lord "sealed the deal," so to speak. He met me again on this subject in a beautiful way when I was watching the movie, "One Night with the King." I love this movie because I love the book of Esther. I was watching the most intense part of the movie. Esther was about to approach the king unannounced. She walked down the long aisle dead center of the room. All eyes were on her. The room was full of men, I might add. They watched her every move. Fear must have flooded the place. No one knew what her fate would be. Would the king reject her presence? Would he receive her by extending his scepter? During this intense scene, I heard The Lord whisper, "You can come to me like that, Becky, and you don't have to be afraid." I broke to pieces in sobbing tears.

We can go to Him without fear. He will not

reject us. The Bible says that He was rejected and despised by men. **(Isaiah 53)** He took on Himself all rejection and even the fear of rejection so we would not have to. We are welcome to come boldly to the throne of grace so we can obtain mercy and find grace in a time of need. **(Hebrew 4:16)** The Lord accepts us. He extended His scepter, His cross, a long time ago. We can go to Him.

*May The Lord come to you, driving out every thought and emotion rooted in rejection. Be at peace and do not fear. God will not reject you. He will only welcome you to come near.*

**From Pitiful to Beautiful-Walk Blessed!**

    Several years ago, I had a dream. Jacob, the son of Isaac, came to my house. **(Genesis 25)** I saw him walk into my backyard. When I woke up, I knew I was in for another journey. I have shared about The Lord healing the pain of rejection in my heart, how He caused my thought pattern to change and caused me to recognize my enemy. Now, He was taking me deeper. The Lord taught me how rejection had been working in my life and how to keep it out as I read the story of Jacob. It's been a battle, but The Lord has been faithful.

    To paraphrase, Jacob was loved by his mother, and his twin brother Esau was loved by their father. **(Genesis 25:28)** Esau was to inherit the birthright and the blessing, not Jacob. I believe this left him feeling rejected and caused him to do things he wouldn't normally do. I think it pushed Jacob to want more, to seek approval, seek affirmation, and seek all he could get his hands on. As you read his life story, you'll find that he wanted the blessing and seemed to stop at nothing to get it. **(Genesis 25-33.)**

So, where do we find ourselves? Wanting more blessings! We want to be accepted. We want to be chosen. Though we are sons and daughters blessed by God already, we don't always know that. As we search for it, we don't always recognize what is already around us.

The enemy will throw anything at us he can to stop us from knowing God's love for us. Satan taunts us and deceives us into believing God is not good, He doesn't want us, and that there's *no* blessing to obtain. He will move us to do things we usually would not do and when we fail—more rejection! It becomes a never-ending cycle. We can't force anyone into a relationship with us. We can't make our promotions happen. We can't make anyone love us. We will only find ourselves crossing a line and getting hurt with more rejection. Look, rejections will come. Wrong things happen. I am not saying they don't. Some are intentional and some are not. Jacob felt it. So will we. There is rejection when there is a divorce, abandonment, abuse, job loss, and other life happenings.

Accepting the fact that rejection happens, helped me to overcome the pain that came with it. How? I learned to acknowledge it, rise above it, and move on. I paid attention to my bad thoughts and pushed them out of my mind. I chose to overcome rejection. God shows me His love. He accepts me, affirms me, and blesses me every day. I choose to embrace that.

Jacob wanted his blessing; he sought it and obtained it. I want mine too. I remind myself of how blessed I am. I walk with God, and I choose to spend time with Him every day. Just like Jacob walked in my backyard a blessed man, so will I, and so can you.

*Though rejection happens, it does not define us. It does not define our heavenly Father either. God loves you.*

**From Pitiful to Beautiful-Desire of All Nations!**

As the journey of rejection continued, the Lord spoke more to me through the life of Jacob. **(Genesis 25-33)** During Jacob's search for the blessing, He deceived people and wrestled with God. He deceived his father and brother and ran away. He continued to struggle in life.

This story opened my eyes. Rejection and "wrongdoings" really will happen in life. The struggles are real. I believed if I chose to do right, then everyone around me would choose to do the same. It just doesn't happen like that. We can be rejected and wounded with the "rejecter" being oblivious to what they have done. We all make mistakes. We all have different opinions, preferences, and perspectives. Honestly, sometimes people will reject you on purpose; they can be mean.

Rejection had ruled me and robbed my joy

many times. I "felt" rejected and unwanted regularly. The rejection became a pattern in my mind and emotions until God healed my pain. Not only did He heal me, but He exposed my enemy. Exposing the way rejection worked has been a genuine treasure from God. It enabled me to fight and win.

I found that the deeper the wound of rejection and the longer it's been there, the more the person strives to be accepted. They will crave honor, flattery, position, and prestige. They want to be noticed.

When wounded with rejection, you will carry it in your presence. People will feel rejected by you simply because of the way you present yourself. In turn, they reject you, and the cycle continues.

Rejection can be a powerful catalyst for "man pleasing". Some will go to the extreme of wanting to be exalted. These things all seem prideful because they are. Pride is the medicine Satan offers for your pain. Rejection can become a very dangerous enemy.

The Bible teaches us that Jesus is the "Desire of All Nations." **(Haggai 2:7)** When I read this passage it leads me to believe we are much like Jacob. We have a desire for God! We want Him to bless us. We want to know Him and His love. We want affirmation and acceptance. As Jacob wrestled with God, we can find ourselves doing the same. **(Genesis 32)** He wrestled until God blessed him. In that moment, everything changed for Jacob, even his name. He became a new man, a man of peace. Jacob became a man *knowing* God blesses him, instead of a man *wrestling* to be blessed by God. Let's learn by his example.

I had to learn not to respond to rejection by acknowledging God's love for me. I prayed for love to grow in my heart. There were times I felt so unwanted that I needed God to convince me that He wanted me and loved me. I was determined to beat this. Faithfully, He's doing that. Now, rejection has little effect on my emotions.

We must catch this one Truth **"God so loved the world that He gave His only begotten Son that whosoever would believe in Him would not perish but have everlasting life." John 3:16.** The keywords to this truth: God so loved the world. He loves all of us. How much more blessed can we be?

*May the Desire of All Nations overtake you, filling your heart with love and affirmation.*

**From Pitiful to Beautiful-Rise above it!**

Rejection and betrayal are not the same. We can believe the inner pain we feel is from the rejection we encountered. That may not be true. Rejection does hurt and can do a number on the emotions; it did mine. But betrayal carries a deeper purpose. Betrayal burns the bridge of a relationship, leaving you empty and broken. It destroys trust. Knowing the difference between the two is important. I must say, "Know who your enemy is." You will fight better.

We are going to get rejected and we are going to reject others. We may not mean to, but it is impossible not to. I've been on both sides of the fence here. Various reasons cause the sting of rejection. We can't expect everyone to agree with us. Sometimes we are left out. We do not get invited to all the events. There are those that will not be mindful enough to reach out to us. Others will not offer a helping hand. I know from experience that rejection cuts deep and causes a lot of heartaches. We cannot embrace rejection. Rejection of any kind will lie like a heavy weight on your spirit and open you to extreme emotional problems. Don't give the devil place.

Betrayal is planned. It happens between you and someone you have a relationship with. It is schemes and plots made against you. Plans were made behind your back, and they were hurtful to you. Betrayal is typically thought out. When someone has betrayed you, they intentionally made plans. An affair in a marriage is an intentional betrayal; lies were told. If you own a business and your employee robs you, it is betrayal because of the trust you had with the employee. The bottom line is this; a betrayer breaks the bond of trust.

How do we recover from that? Look at the life of Joseph. Read Genesis 37 through 50 and ask The Lord to speak to you. The Bible teaches us that when Joseph's brothers betrayed him, he extended to them mercy and forgiveness.

His brothers plotted to get rid of him because they were jealous. They sold him into slavery and lied to their father and said that a wild animal killed him. See the pattern? Plans. Plots. Lies.

Joseph got through this betrayal. It took time, and sometimes we need that. Step by step and season after season, Joseph succeeded in life. The Lord worked forgiveness in Joseph's heart and caused him to be the one to save his family-the very ones who betrayed Him! Forgiveness and mercy healed Joseph's heart and His family. His life's account is a beautiful story.

Do we have to trust our betrayer? No. I don't believe so. The Bible doesn't teach that. However, it teaches us to forgive, be merciful, and learn that the Lord's ways are perfect. **"As for God, His way is perfect; The word of the Lord is proven; He is a shield to all who trust in Him." 2 Samuel 22:31.** We can trust God! In Joseph's case, a family was saved and healed as he trusted God and followed His way. That's all that is required. Trust God.

*May every pain in your heart from betrayal (received or given) be healed in Jesus name! Follow God and trust His way!*

**From Pitiful to Beautiful-Walk Softly!**

I heard a song in my ear years ago. I kept hearing it over and over in my spirit. **"Saul has slain his thousands, but David his ten thousands." 1 Samuel 18:7b** I didn't understand at the time that I was going to find myself in a very painful situation that lasted several years. I don't know how I made it, other than I prayed a lot, and I did my best to follow David's example, honor. I just honored the best I knew how. I *walked softly,* so to speak. I didn't walk everything out in excellence but did my very best. In time, God delivered me from that season and healed my heart. I am forever thankful.

Sometimes betrayal breaks a relationship, but that relationship can be restored, just like Joseph and his brothers. There are also times that it will not be restored, like with Saul and David **(1 Samuel 17-31).** As Christians, we should follow examples written in God's Word and follow the Holy Spirit's guidance through these situations. We should learn to forgive, reconcile, walk softly, and even walk away.

The Scriptures say that King Saul had appointed David to be over the men of war. David victoriously slew Goliath (their enemy), so King Saul made him the leader of his army. David was a great warrior. People loved and admired him so much that the women would sing, **"Saul has slain his thousands, but David his ten thousands." (1 Sam. 18:7b)** Saul became angry and jealous of this. He "eyed" David from that day forward.

Saul tried to kill David, but David would escape every time. Saul feared him because he knew the Lord was with David and was no longer with him. There was a continual plot to kill David. Saul was jealous and constantly scheming against David. Saul moved deceitfully by giving his daughter to David to marry, asking David to fight for him in return. The marriage was only in hopes of seeing David killed at war. Betrayal. Betrayal. Betrayal.

David was not like Saul. Yes, he had opportunities to kill Saul, but he did not. The Bible says David was a man after God's heart. **(1 Sam. 13:14)** He chose to walk in honor (softly) concerning King Saul. David knew God had anointed him to be the new King but waited patiently on God and honored the present King. That's God's way of handling these things. Give honor.

There were times that David's men had the opportunity to kill Saul, but David would not allow it. Betrayal wasn't in David's heart. Saul was his father-in-law and King. David had a heart after God! Eventually, David did become King, but only after a season of "walking softly."

David chose to walk in honor and not repay evil for evil. That took a lot of humility. He yielded to God, keeping His "eye" on God, just as we must do. We cannot fall to evil if we want the Lord's Presence upon us. We must choose to follow the ways of the Lord, regardless of what others may choose. Pray for them? Yes. Walk softly? Yes. Repay evil for evil? No!

*May The Lord grant us the grace of humility, keeping us diligent in His ways! Honor God and do not repay evil with evil. The Lord's PRESENCE be upon you!*

**From Pitiful to Beautiful-He Sees All!**

I had a dream that I was in heaven. I saw Jesus lying flat on His back with outstretched arms. His body was humongous; He was massive and breath-taking! His chest was thick and muscular. He was as long as an entire city. He was an incredible sight to see. I saw people coming from everywhere; they were walking into His body. They were walking into the piercing in His side. He laid there as the people walked up to Him and in Him. I knew they were walking straight into His heart. It was so beautiful.

As I was walking up to The Lord, I was crying, wailing, almost hysterically. I could not go into Him; I wanted to but couldn't make myself. I was crying loudly, "I can't give myself to you like this! I can't give *You* all of me! I just can't, not like this!" I was sobbing hard. I could barely speak out my words. I wanted to give myself entirely to

Christ, but I was aware of the ugliness of my filth.

I heard a voice say to me, "When I see you, I see pitiful!" Ouch, that hurt! The Lord sees everything. He even sees how we see ourselves. When I woke up, I knew The Lord wasn't calling me pitiful. He was revealing to me the view I had of myself. He saw the "pitiful" I believed I was. When we bring ourselves to The Lord, we bring our whole being. We bring our attitudes, thoughts, emotions, beliefs, and deceptions. He sees it all. I could hardly believe it. Did I believe I was in that bad of shape? I wondered about the "pitiful" I thought was me. What was this? I found myself on another journey of healing. I needed more freedom. The enemy was "self-pity."

In my own experience, I came to learn some essential truths about this challenging deception. Such as, self-pity can begin with a kind of abuse, injustice, or painful rejection. It is a horrible feeling of despair and pain. Self-pity is not limited to feeling sorry for yourself. Everyone does that from time to time. It carries a deep inner pain that convinces you that there is no way out of your pain. It is extreme hopelessness. Thoughts like "My problems are way too big to be fixed, so I'm trapped" and thoughts like, "My pain is too deep and too strong, no one can help me" are from self-pity. It sees the extreme, making mountains out of molehills. That type of sadness is a horrible heaviness that can't be shaken. For me, it was what many people would call depression.

People tormented with self-pity also battle with self-hate and self-rejection. I found that out along the way. I know that you can be deceived into hating and rejecting yourself because you believe that God and others feel the same way. You do not love yourself or who you are. Sadly, this can go to the extreme of hurting yourself or taking your own life.

Self-pity causes you to keep God at a distance. Out of fear, you don't want God to see the person you believe you are. This fear causes you to believe that He will reject you and that God doesn't care for you. But in reality, He already knows what you believe and how you feel. Your thoughts and emotions are not hidden from Him. He is God.

Jesus willingly died on the cross for you. He wants you to come near. He loves you, and with great compassion, desires to heal you and set you free from self-pity. We are all welcome to come to Him and in Him. Jesus welcomes us into His heart. God greatly loves us!

After that dream, I sought to know God even more. I became acutely aware that I was a complete mess and needed help. The Lord was the only One I thought might have the power to help me. Notice I said might. There were times I doubted. Still, I chose to trust God because I had nowhere else to turn. He has never let me down and He won't let you down either. Choose Him and give Him your pain. Jesus died for you. What greater love is that?

***Greater love has no one than this, than to lay down one's life for his friends. John 15:13.*** *Jesus loves you.*

**From Pitiful to Beautiful-For Your Good!**

I understand some would say depression is a chemical imbalance or a hormonal imbalance. That may be so in some cases. For me, it was not. My emotional state affected my mental state, and my thoughts affected my emotions. This could have affected me physically, but I can't say that for sure. I was all mixed up. All I know is once self-pity left me, the symptoms of depression left too.

There comes a time when you get sick of living the life you are living. You tire of the anger, pain, and sadness. I wasn't sure if anyone had ever beaten self-pity, but I was going to try. I followed The Lord the best way I knew and learned all I could from Him. I believe in "going down one way and coming up another," but I was aware this was another journey. It was going to take some time.

Self-pity is rooted in pride. It begins with the word "self." It undoubtedly has you focused on yourself. It's about how you feel, how you are treated, and how things affect you. You. You. You. Self-pity convinces you that you are messed up, and your problems are so big that no one could deal with all the baggage you carry. It is to say, "I want help, but cannot see the possibility of getting help." Self-pity is self-centered and filled with hopelessness.

We can believe we should never suffer a wrong. Boy, oh boy, that's a trap! That's where I fell. I felt right was right and wrong was wrong. If I knew to choose right and do right, then so should everyone else. I had a high value for justice and was appalled at an injustice. This belief led me to believe I was a mere victim. I was an angry one at that!

We can believe we are victims of people, circumstances, and even illnesses. Have you ever heard anyone say, "Well, it never fails, if anyone is going to get something, it's going to be me" or "Why does everything bad have to happen to me?" Yes, it is self-pity getting its hold in your mind. If it remains, it will lead you into a deep depression. This is where I would fall. I wanted to do right, be treated right, and wanted everything to go right. Life does not always happen that way, but I expected it to.

The Bible says, **"And we know that all things work together for good to those who love**

**God, and to those who are the called according to His purposes." Romans 8:28** Give things time to "work." Everything doesn't end suddenly, and it doesn't always go the way we plan. Bad things happen, but don't get hung up there. Do not give place to disappointment. I made the mistake of not allowing time for anything to work out. I would either get angry or fall to self-pity believing there was no way out of my situation. Hopelessness would set in. You know what? That made things worse, and it gave place to the enemy. I couldn't emotionally handle the slightest trouble. I had no patience. I made mountains out of molehills because I focused on me, how things would affect me, instead of focusing on God and believing Him to work things out for my good.

***Wait on The Lord; Be of good courage, And he shall strengthen your heart; Wait, I say, on the Lord! Psalms 27:14.*** *Give Him time to work things out.*

**From Pitiful to Beautiful-On Things Above**

I remember being stretched out across my bed, face down, feeling heavy in spirit, confused and afraid. I kept seeing an evil face when I closed my eyes. It was a moment of awful torment. I was praying and asking God to help me. I couldn't shake it by myself; I knew I needed Him!

I heard The Lord say firmly, "Look at me Becky, look at me." As I tried to focus on The Lord and heaven, I could feel some relief. As time went on, I realized the importance of not focusing on myself and things that are only about me, but on *things above.* **"If then you were raised with Christ, seek those things which are above, where Christ is, sitting at the right hand of God. Set your mind on things above, not on things on the earth." (Colossians 3:1-2)**

When I focused on myself, my soulish desires, and how I felt, I was focused merely on me, myself, and I. This pride had to go. This mindset of "self" had to be torn down. It was a catalyst that caused me to fall into self-pity (depression if you will). One can get focused on themselves to the point of becoming *soul-sick* and remaining in bed for days. I had not fallen that deep into the *dark hole* of self-pity, but I know those that have. It's a horrible snare from the enemy that causes significant emotional pain. I was close and was fighting with all I had in me.

When we focus, meditate, and rehearse all the things that have hurt us or made us mad, we suffer emotionally. We must remember that love does not keep a record of *wrongs.* **(1 Cor. 13)** Love believes all things, hopes all things, and bears all things. It bears you up. Love covers a multitude of sins, both those we commit and those committed against us. Focus, meditate, and rehearse that. Focus on heavenly things, the things of God.

Self-seeking, self-centeredness, and taking account of everything *done wrong* to you are prideful. These are the opposites of love. Love gives up self and takes on Christ's image by dying to selfish ways and expectations. When God said to me, "focus on ME Becky," He was saying, "focusing on yourself instead of *Me* is a trap." There will be challenging and painful things to happen in your life. Falling into self-pity will not rescue you. It will not save anyone else either. It does the opposite. It keeps you focused on you, trapping you in the pain of the event. We must refocus.

Because self-pity *emotions* are real and painful events have genuinely occurred, there is a deception in believing the *emotions* (feelings) of self-pity are normal. We must be careful with our thinking because these feelings are not normal. They result from something and are influenced by tormenting spirits that are not from God but from the devil.

We can have emotional pain that is not self-pity. It is normal to feel. When the pain lingers and becomes hopelessness and despair, there is usually a problem. Knowing the difference is vital.

Lie across your bed and pray to God, ask for His help. Ask The Lord to remove self-pity from you and the emotions attached to it. He will set you free and show you things from above.

*May Christ rule and reign in our hearts, causing us to live free from all pain. Take time each day to focus on Him.*

**From Pitiful to Beautiful-You Know my Heart!**

Another struggle I had was feeling like I had done something "wrong." I always felt guilty! Guilt controlled a significant portion of my life. I was continually repenting for every little thing. I would ask God for forgiveness for things I did not do—what if I did not remember them? I questioned if I even knew Him, was I even saved?

I was moved by guilt daily. I could not say *no.* When I was asked to do something or take part in something, I felt like I had to. If I said *no,* guilt would consume me. I did things I did not want to do and did not need to do. I thought I had to say *yes* because that would show I had a good heart. My thoughts were, "If my heart is right with God, I will do what others ask." Not sinful things, of course, but simple everyday tasks. I thought I was being kind and showing love when I said *yes.* If I said *no,* because I honestly did not want to, guilt would cause me to have anxiety and panic attacks.

I often thought to myself, "What am I doing wrong now?" It was a question frequently on my mind. When life seemed to go in the wrong direction, I would question what I did wrong. When I was sick, having anxiety, or if something hurtful happened, I questioned if I was being punished. I had convinced myself that I did something wrong. Guilt plagued my mind. When I would pray, I would ask God, "What did I do? Where did I open the door to the enemy?" Instead of searching *where* the guilt came from or *who* made me feel this guilt, I searched for what *I* did wrong. What a trap!

Another problem I had with guilt was the inability to accept correction. Correction made me feel condemned. I did not understand that correction and discipline from The Lord would help me. I received it as a statement that said, "Once again, you have done wrong!" Guilt would overwhelm me. I would feel blamed instead of helped. In turn, I would find myself blaming others. I could not handle any more bad thoughts. Guilt wore me out.

One day a man of God mentioned to me 1 John, which seemed to be out of the blue. It caught my attention, though. So, I began to study it. **"My little children let us not love in word or in tongue but, in deed and in truth. And by this we know that *we are of the truth* and shall assure our hearts before Him. For if our hearts condemns** us, *God is greater than our heart*, **and knows all things." 1 John 3:18-20** (emphasis added)

As I read my Bible, I heard the Holy Spirit say, "What are your intentions, Becky?" I said, "I want to love well, do well, and choose what is right and pleasing to you. I wholeheartedly want to be honest, pure, and clean." Then He said, "So you're not guilty!" Wow! God looks at the heart and He knew mine. I wasn't guilty!?! My heart's intentions were good. I may have *felt* condemned, but God is much greater than how I *feel*. He knows me better than I know myself. He knows I desperately want to be right with Him.

That moment changed me forever. The Lord knows our hearts even when we don't. Thank you, God! He knows your intentions and weighs them far more than your mistakes. **"For the Lord does not see as man sees; for man looks at the outward appearance, but The Lord looks at the heart" 1 Sam. 16:7b**

*May The Lord visit you, revealing your heart to you! May guilt leave your thought life and may peace that comes with the Assurance of Heaven flood your soul! May His Love define you!*

**From Pitiful to Beautiful-Justice Served!**

    I must say, The Lord is full of wisdom and power. He knows how to rescue us from our history. You may think that it is impossible to be rescued from your past, but that is not entirely true. It really can be wiped clean. Totally.

    The Lord started visiting me on things I regretted. He would do that in different ways. The Lord would give me dreams and visions of things I did not want to deal with and did not want to remember. He would bring to my remembrance things that happened in my past. I wouldn't say I enjoyed it, but now I know I needed it. I needed to allow myself to remember. I needed to interact with the dreams and the memories so I could be healed. I was robbed of my joy and was left fearful and anxious. I wanted to be healed.

    I asked the Holy Spirit to lead me to my healing. I wanted my joy back. I did not know how to deal with the past, but I had to believe that He did. As I dreamed of past situations, I would walk through the dream because I wanted to put an end to it; I had to face it. I made an intentional choice to walk through it. Before, I would run in fear but not anymore. I would face an event and say, "Ok, I did this, but I'm not doing it now. That's over. I'm not like that anymore." That brought me a lot of healing.

At times, my dreams and memories were based on things others did to me or things they said to me. I would tell myself "But that is over. I made it. It's not happening now." My heart would then forgive and let it all go. Everyone makes mistakes. Some even do things on purpose, but it's still over and gone. It's history! **"For I The Lord love justice; and I hate robbery for burnt offering; I will direct their work in truth, and will make with them an everlasting covenant." Isaiah 61:8** I lived this scripture. The Lord directed my work forward and healed me with the truth. As the Holy Spirit led me, I became free. I repented, forgave and justice was served!

Today is a new day. Yesterday was yesterday. We can live free of regrets by yielding to the Holy Spirit and asking Him to lead us into healing. We may not want to confront the conflict inside ourselves, but we need to so we can be healed. Whether you find yourself facing it in dreams or in your quiet time, face it. No one likes fear or anxiety. We desire peace, joy, and freedom, but there comes a time when we must confront our history. The truth will lead the way!

*May The Lord lead you in your coming days. He will direct your work in truth leading you to freedom.*

**From Pitiful to Beautiful-Covenant Keeper**

I loved hearing, "You are in covenant with me, Becky." I heard this when I was in a battle with depression and high anxiety. I am grateful these words flowed straight from heaven and into my ears. I can rejoice, for my name is written in HEAVEN!

When the enemy throws doubt, confusion, and fear your way remember you belong to Jesus. We are in a blood covenant with The Lord Jesus Christ. You are under the blood and all its power! Just stop and think, *ALL IT'S POWER*!!! I can enjoy the forgiveness of all my sins and then relax knowing that I have a powerful future in Him.

Nowhere have I found in scripture that I have to walk a fine line or else God will whack me. Sometimes I think Christians develop the wrong view of God. The enemy lies continuously, wanting us to believe that God is not good and that we are not safe with Him. Sometimes the devil causes us to question if we are truly saved.

The Bible tells us, **"If we confess our sins, The Lord is faithful and just to forgive us all our sins and to cleanse us from all unrighteousness." 1 John 1:9** Amen! All we have to do is talk to The Lord about it? Yes. Once we go as far as confession, we've gone as far as true repentance. Being sincere and going to Him for help is all He requires for the blood to wash it all away. It's that simple.

For years I let the enemy torment me with my every wrong. The wrongdoings of my past, present, and what I might do in the future. What a snare of fear! I felt like I had to walk a fine line. Somehow, I had by-passed the "paths of righteousness." A path is much wider than a fine line. I don't have to be perfect; I only have to follow Him. He will do the rest. **"The Lord is my shepherd; I shall not want. He makes me to lie down in green pastures; He leads me beside still waters. He restores my soul; He leads me in the paths of righteousness for His name's sake." Psalm 23:1-3**

Thank you, God, for your Word! Our God will lead us our entire life! We are in covenant with Him. He will guide us all the way through. We can lean into Him to restore our souls, our minds, and our emotions. Jesus leads with peace on the paths of righteousness. Jesus is who we belong to!

*May The Lord reveal to your heart the covenant that you are in with Him! May the precious blood of the Lamb become more real to you!*

**From Pitiful to Beautiful-Believing Him!**

**"Beloved, if our hearts do not condemn us, we have confidence toward God." 1 John 3:21.** I was not always confident in my relationship with God, not that my relationship with Him was not good. I mean my confidence was not there. I had the wrong kind of fear working in me through guilt. Fear enabled the enemy to influence areas of my life. I believed the enemy's lies and fell into an awful trap. I needed to believe God was *Who* His Word said He was.

    I was moved by guilt when others would manipulate me into giving them what they wanted. I was afraid not to because I thought it was wrong to say "no." So, I did what was asked of me. One way the enemy works against us is through others. Maybe they did not realize what they were doing. It is possible that they wanted what they wanted, regardless of how they would get it.

Be careful if you are prone to respond with guilt. You will fall, giving in every time. Giving-in is not God's way. Our relationship with God is not about *giving* others what they want but *giving* our life to God. He will direct us in what we are to give to others. Don't allow others to wear you out.

As a parent, guilt tormented me over my children. I felt entirely responsible for them. I would plead the blood of Jesus over them every day through grade school and middle school. It was the right thing to do and God blessed my kids. However, if they did wrong or something went wrong, I would feel guilty and then believed I did not pray enough for them. I thought the choices they made were solely a result of me and my relationship with God. Ugh. I was so wrong. I do believe as parents we are the most significant influence in our children's lives, but they make their own choices.

The Bible says, **"A child is known by his deeds, whether what he does is pure and right." Proverbs 20:11** Simply put, it means they make choices of their own. My job is to believe God heard my prayers and that He would do what He said He would in His Word. I have to believe that all His promises are "yes and amen!"

"A child known by his deeds" was highlighted to me after I had a troubling dream. I saw a young teenager that was close to my son standing in a hallway. He was standing by a closed door and thinking about going through it. The door led to a bad place, and I knew it. I pleaded with him not to walk through the door, but he did anyway. When I woke up, I felt guilty because I knew him. Had I not prayed enough? Should I have said something to him? I started feeling responsible. Here is where The Lord spoke Proverbs 20:11 to me. It gave me peace, though I hurt for that young man and wished I could have stopped him. I thought of my children. I hope they choose well. I can't decide for them, but I can pray for them and believe God to answer.

We cannot feel guilty about everything. It moves us to fear, and fear is not faith. I had to learn to be at peace and *believe* God. That is faith. Our children will make mistakes and so will their friends. Being sick with fear and anxiety because we feel guilty has no positive effect. It will not help them to make better choices, and it has a very negative impact. Fear stops the flow of peace we need in challenging situations and will hinder our faith we need to fight.

**"Let us hold fast the confession of our hope without wavering, for He who promised is faithful." Hebrews 10:23** Guilt causes us to waver and it critically weakens us. We must recognize it and rid it from our lives. For some, it is the force driving anxiety and panic attacks. Excessive worry (anxiety) can be fear caused by guilt. We will doubt

God's faithfulness when we believe His faithfulness depends on *our actions*. Truth is *Faithful* is who He is regardless of our actions. He can handle our children all on His own. We must believe Him!

*May all seeds of guilt planted in your heart come out now! May the God of peace visit you with the confidence of "He is Faithful" all the days of your life, in Jesus name!*

**From Pitiful to Beautiful-Heaven's Angels!**

It was a hard day. This day I am sharing with you took place several years ago. I was having one of the worst days of panic attacks ever. I went for a walk and prayed. I set out on my back deck and prayed. Then, I stretched across my bed face-down and prayed. I didn't know what else to do. So, I waited on God.

I remember it was a bright summer day. The sun shined all day long. Everything around me was beautiful. My children were healthy and beautiful, my husband had a well-paying job, and I loved our little house. But, on the inside, I was falling apart and in desperate need of help.

I was on a journey with The Lord that would lead me to total healing. This moment in time is etched in my memory and I'll never forget it. As I lay stretched out across my bed, I heard a voice say to me, "Go see your doctor, Becky." I hesitated, stunned by what I heard. See a doctor? Wait, can I actually do that? I just waited for a second and listened for this voice again. I was questioning who was speaking. She (the voice sounding feminine) didn't say anything more.

I could feel peace in her voice. Her voice was gentle and soothing. She sounded similar to a dear grandmother I know who has a soft, soothing voice. However, this "voice" sounded young. I knew it wasn't The Lord but wandered who she was. I knew she was from heaven; I could trust what she said because of the "weighty peace" in the room. I sensed the presence of heaven. I did see my doctor and I have never regretted that decision. He helped me for a season, and I am thankful.

I had a couple of experiences with the "voice" I heard that day. Over time, I learned that she is an angel. I believe she is assigned to me; to help me through life as The Lord instructs her. **"For He shall give His angels charge over you, to keep you in all your ways." Psalms 91:11** Because of the feminine sound of her voice and seeing her as a woman, I call her a "she."

Later, I saw her in a dream. I knew it was her. I recognized her voice. She was ministering to me while I was lying on a stretcher. She was dressed in a white nursing uniform (a dress, not scrubs) and she wore a white nurse's hat. She had bright red hair and a beautiful round face. Her complexion looked like porcelain. I asked, "Are you always with me?" She said, "yes."

I am thankful for guardian angels! God never leaves us without help. Not only is His Holy Spirit living inside of us, but He assigns angels to be with us always. How blessed we are to have such gifts from our God!

*May The Lord bless you with the awareness of heaven's Angels! Know that you are never alone, and you are never without help. We have a GOOD GOD that gives us good gifts!*

**From Pitiful to Beautiful-Spirit Lead Me!**

During a season when my mind was racing and screaming, "I don't know what else to do," I yielded more to the Holy Spirit. There comes a time where we need to say, "I give up!" I don't mean fall away from the path The Lord has us on, what I mean is, stop trying to figure it out and go with the flow. That's difficult for those suffering from an emotional disorder; I understand. We need control because we fear sinking. Let me explain.

I was at church one Sunday morning, some years ago. I was so tired with panic attacks. It was all I could do to muster up enough strength to go anywhere. My days were stressful and near a breaking point. I struggled to keep composure; to maintain control. My nights were long and dreadful, and I could hardly sleep for wrestling with anxiety. It was just a rough battle.

During that worship service, I felt the wind

of the Holy Spirit around my feet. I had a desire to dance my heart out. I didn't know why that came upon me, but it did. Now, mind you that no one was dancing for The Lord. We were only singing to God and praising Him in song. I didn't think about if I should take off dancing or why I should dance. I just "gave up" and went with it. Thank God I did! The anointing was released in the room and cooperate worship went to another level. But most of all, I went to another level!

Just like King David, I continued to dance in worship before the Lord! **"Then David danced before The Lord with all his might, and David was wearing a linen ephod." 2 Samuel 6:14** I noticed I was getting stronger and stronger in overcoming the anxiety. So, I just kept dancing when I worshiped God. I know now that The Lord led me into "dancing in the Spirit" as a weapon against my enemy. "Dancing" has become one of my weapons when I'm in a spiritual battle. Holy Spirit led me to that point because He never leaves us without help.

Sometime around that season, I had an encounter with my angel again. I was sitting on my front porch in a swing. I must have been praying or waiting on The Lord because I suddenly noticed The Lord sitting on the swing beside me!! All I could do was bawl like a baby! I remember gently leaning in on His shoulder as He comforted me. I continued to sob.

That's when I saw my angel, just as I had before, in a white nursing uniform and a white nurse's hat. She was sitting on my porch banister. Seeing her just sitting there startled me at first and I thought, "OH no, what am I in for, now?" I thought this because I generally see her when warfare is at its peak. As she came toward me, I looked down at my feet and noticed shackles and chains. She came over to me and took them off! I cried more.

Obviously, "dancing in the Spirit" set me free at another level. Honestly, I cannot remember if my angel took away the shackles before or after I started dancing. However, I remember that season released me into another breakthrough, and I became stronger.

*Spirit, lead us where our trust is without borders! Send angels to minister to us and may we learn just to let go and let God!*

***but the greatest of these is love." 1 Corinthians 13:13*** *May your faith in Jesus grow.*

**From Pitiful to Beautiful-The River!**

Throughout the years, I have dreamed of a river. This river is massive and fierce. The more I think upon it, "majestic" would better describe it. Though it is beautiful, it terrified me, especially the rapids. This river scared me. I felt that I needed to jump in and enjoy it but couldn't get myself to do it. Now there were times I would dip the tips of my toes in it. There were times I would jump in just for a second in the shallow parts. I even found myself on large rocks in the middle of this river, trying my best to get out of it. Fear always stopped me from enjoying these majestic waters. I dreamed of it often.

When I would wake up from these dreams, I knew the river was representing God. I knew that if I could dive in and enjoy the river that it would mean I was surrendering to His Spirit. As long as I resisted the river and feared it, I was actually resisting Him and fearing Him wrongly. It merely meant that I did not trust that The Lord was safe. These dreams were not about the water but about trusting God with my life. I was afraid, the kind that kept me from God. It was the opposite of the "Fear of The Lord," which draws us to Him.

We can wrongly think that the closer we get to the "spiritual" things the scarier God is. To be honest, the closer we get to Him, the safer we will find Him to be. We will find *His peace* and *His joy* as we draw near. The closer we get to Him, the more we fall in love with Him. Yes, there is fear in The Lord, but you invite it, not avoid it. His fear cleanses, excites, and inspires us to run even harder after Him because of *Who* He is.

God wants us to experience Him as He invites us into the most intimate parts of His heart, but first, we must overcome fear. We have to plunge in despite our fears! Jumping in is what I had to do. I believe the fear of the rapids in this river has said, "You fear the unknown." We must surrender and trust. It took me a while to do that. If I could not see that it was safe, I was not willing to take the risk. It became clear to me that my faith needed to grow.

One night before falling to sleep, I prayed and asked God to help me embrace the river. I wanted to relax and enjoy it. I knew it would be a breakthrough in fear if I could. Again, I dreamed about the river. Massive. Fierce. Rapid. Majestic. As the wind blew, I stood looking out at its beauty, wanting to dive in. But I was stuck. I could not move. Then suddenly, I soared over the river, and I got a closer look. Wow, this massive river was not only beautiful, but it was knee-deep! Really?! How safe is that?

When I woke up, I could hardly believe it. With such beautiful imagery, The Lord showed me how safe He was and caused joy to rise in my heart. How could I not trust a God, the One that would meet me in my dreams, lift me above the fear, so that I could rest in His loving arms of peace? **"Have I not commanded you? Be of good courage; do not be afraid, nor be dismayed, for The Lord your God is with you wherever you go?" Joshua 1:9** He truly loves us and wants us to enjoy all of Him!

*May The Lord meet you where you are, causing you to rise above every fear, finding that place of peace that causes your faith to grow mightily in Him! Trust Him. He's safe.*

*Prayers~ Thoughts~ Impressions*

**From Pitiful to Beautiful-Maturity is Power!**

God fully loves us and desires to see His bride made perfect in His love. Is it possible to be made perfect? Yes, it is. To be made perfect means to become mature. It is a mature bride that The Lord Jesus desires, one that is spotless and without blemish. A bride with His power!

I asked The Lord, "How do we release your power?" "How do we obtain it?" I believe the same power that raised Christ from the dead lives in us and that God has given us power over sin, sickness, disease, and everything the enemy throws at us. I want to walk consistently in it.

In a dream, The Lord was showing me passages of scripture. I was reading through them when The Lord wrote a sentence on a sheet of paper. "Maturity is the path to my power." His Words captured my heart. I began sobbing as He revealed this to me. I knew this meant "mature in love."

As I searched this out, I was led to **John 17:23. "I in them, and You in Me, that they may be *made perfect* in one, and that the world may know that You have sent Me, and *loved them as You have loved Me*."** (emphasis added) Jesus prayed that we would be made perfect (mature) in His love! Of all the things for Jesus to pray for us, He prayed that we would have a mature love! In unity? Yes. In union? Yes. But where? In Him, in the Father, through the Spirit in *love!*

The Holy Spirit is given to us to empower us. The Bible says Holy Spirit will guide us into truth, tell us things to come, and He will glorify and declare Christ to us. He will reveal and work the love of God in our hearts, bringing us to maturity. What a powerful plan! His love is vital.

Love covers a multitude of sins, as I previously said, it's the sins I committed, and the sins committed against me. There's nothing in this world with that kind of power. Love believes, love hopes, and love bears all things. Love will bear you up and give you the power to overcome your darkest days. Love flowing out of you will empower you to bear someone else up, helping them through their darkest days. Those days could be sickness, disease, loss, pain, etc. Love lifts us.

Perfect (mature) love will cast out *all* fear. Fear is an enemy, but mature love will cast out *all* fear. Wow! God's power of love that was working in me empowered me to defeat my enemies. I see that more now than ever. I'm not lying-in bed in a dark hole of depression because of His love. I'm not walking the floors with panic attacks because of His love. Somehow, I knew to seek the Love of God, and I am so glad I did. I'm still growing, but thankfully I'm on the right path.

*If Jesus prayed that we would be made perfect (mature) in His love, should we not pray the same? Seek to know the love of God in its fullness. God is love. What's more powerful than that!*

**From Pitiful to Beautiful-The Dance**

There are times, with a grace from heaven; The Lord will draw you to Him so you can experience His love. **"Therefore with loving kindness I have drawn you". Jeremiah 31:3c** I remember getting up one morning at 3:00 am to pack my husband, a coal miner, a lunch for work. After he left, I felt drawn to go to our living room. Usually, I would go back to bed, but not this particular morning.

As I stepped into the living room, I felt the urge to dance for The Lord. I just had such worship and praise come up out of me. It was as though it was being drawn out of me from deep within my spirit. So, I danced for Him. I felt His presence, which gave me a desire to dance for Him and make the dance as beautiful as possible. As I twirled for Him, I sang my love to Him. "Your love is better than wine." **(Song of Songs 4:10)** It was flowing out of my innermost being, so I kept singing.

It was then I could see the Lord in the spirit. He was sitting on my couch watching me. He didn't look exactly like the pictures I had seen of Him, but similar. His hair didn't appear to me to be golden or as long as common pictures portray. His expression was joyful and loving, not sad or sorrowful. Though the details of His appearance were vague, I knew *Who* was there! It was my King! I saw His appearance vaguely but felt the intensity of His presence!

He very much enjoyed my worship. I could feel it. I knew joy was His countenance. I would cry, sing and dance, then cry, sing and dance some more. His presence draws worship out of you. Every bit of love you have for Him effortlessly flows out.

He then got up off the couch and began to dance with me. Shew, I didn't have time to question if this was happening; I just enjoyed it and surrendered to His lead loving every moment in His arms, in His presence! As we were twirling, I sat down on my couch sobbing because I had felt His love for me and the joy He has toward me. As I looked up at Him, He danced for me! What?!? I was wrecked!

"He has a strange rhythm." I thought. I had never seen this before. It reminded me of "the stomping of the grapes" I had seen in a movie once.

It was beautiful yet strong, and there was purpose in every step. He is a magnificent dancer.

I then crashed on the couch, lying there watching Him dance for me, and I was still sobbing. Then, He began to sing! "Your love is better than wine!" My heart felt like it was coming out of my chest and falling on the floor. *I thought I would die.*

Imagine that! Our King says our love for Him is better than wine! Think about this for a moment. Wine was used as the symbol of His blood at The Last Supper Jesus had with His disciples. Wine is often the chosen drink when there is a celebration, such as a wedding. It is usually drunk on a romantic evening with two love birds at an Italian restaurant. Can you see it?

Wine, we can say, is a symbol of love. It's the kind of love that causes you to be completely wrecked in its presence. As we have communion with Him, as we are intimate with Jesus, not only are we in the presence of His love for us, but He is in the presence of our love for Him, and all He has to say is, "Your love is better than wine."

As we embrace His cross and the shedding of His blood, as we fall in love with Him and this precious gift of His love, He sings, "Your Love is better than wine." With the cross of Christ being the most extraordinary love story ever told, and as we draw near to Jesus through His blood, our love is the wine He delights to drink! He found you worth the shedding of His blood.

*Lord, I ask that you would draw the people to you in your loving kindness, pouring out your love for them in song. Drink of His wine and dance!*

**From Pitiful to Beautiful-God is Love!**

    I want to continue to share The Lord's love with you. He passionately wants us all to know His deep love and affection He has for us. Through every test, trial, and hardship, *love* never fails! When I found myself at my lowest, The Lord's love always lifted me and got me through. Remember, His love bears all things (bears you up), believes all things (believes in you), hopes all things (the best for you), and endures all things (for your sake). God is Love. **(John 4:7)**

    Love covers us. **(1 Peter 4:8)** It covers our sins. God covers us! He covers all the "wrongs" that have ever taken place in our lives, and He doesn't stop there. He breaks through when we least expect it and ravishes our hearts with more of His love.

    One evening I was studying the Song of Songs. I was reading **"Let Him kiss me with the kisses of His mouth, for your love is better than**

**wine." (SOS 1:2)** I understood this to mean His breath was touching my breath; His spirit was touching my spirit, intimately. I was overwhelmed with the thoughts of His Spirit touching mine. I remembered "the dance" we had. My love for Him began to rise and flow out of my heart. I wept and said, "I Love You, Lord, I Love You". I kept repeating this over and over. I could feel my words roll off my lips. My breath was warm and soft saying, "I Love You."

Out of nowhere, The Lord quickly descended and came close to my breath and inhaled. He then quickly ascended. I could hardly believe what I saw, although I knew I had encountered Him in that moment. I felt my love for Him flow to Him as I nearly crumbled in His presence!

We often want God to give us something. We want Him to help us and astonish us. Now, I know that love truly goes both ways. He wants something from us too. He wants us to love Him! He wants us to encounter Him! He loves and desires those intimate moments. **"You shall love The Lord your God with all your heart, with all your soul and with all your mind." (Matt 22:37)** He is saying that He wants us to love Him with everything we are.

How precious is the thought of The Lord wanting our love! As little or as much as we have, He has a desire for it. For me, every encounter of

His love causes me to love Him more and more. We love Him because He first loved us! **(1 John 4:19)** His love quiets our souls and causes our spirit to be at peace. Nothing is more remarkable because God is Love!

*May Love visit you tonight, quieting your soul and blessing your spirit with peace! May you give Him all that you are for He loves you and desires you.*

**From Pitiful to Beautiful-Belonging!**

    I want to share another dream with you that The Lord gave me. I was wearing a beautiful pink dress. It was gorgeous, fancy and reminded me of the dress style you would see in the movie "Gone with the Wind." The dress was lined with a perfect amount of white lace around the bust and neckline. It fit me perfectly! I remember looking down. I was pleasantly surprised at how beautiful the dress was with its perfect white lace. I loved it. It made me feel beautiful!

    I looked over to see my husband dressed in a suit. If my recollection is correct, it was black and gray. He, too, looked as if he were from the 1800s. As I saw a scarf wrapped around his neck, neatly tucked in his vest, I thought of REVIVAL. Together we walked across the street to attend a banquet.

    I stepped into the banquet hall; I saw several people. Some I knew, some I didn't recognize.

People were seated, eating their dinner, dressed in their finest apparel. My husband took his seat as I walked across the room to the banqueting table. As I walked, I could feel that all eyes were on me. Usually, I would feel intimidated and embarrassed, but not this time. I felt confidant and courageous, for I knew *Who* I belonged to; I belonged to my husband, who was also my King! I knew *Who's* I was, as did everyone else in the room.

    I stepped up to the banqueting table and thought, **"You prepare a table before me in the presence of my enemies." Psalms 23:5a** I continued down the table, filling my plate with fine foods. I was also looking for foods my husband would like. I felt like royalty as I traveled to that table. I knew it was a great privilege just to be invited to this banquet. I could feel humility and grace resting on me. It kept me at peace. The love that flowed through my spirit felt like sweet, warm rain rushing softly and gently through my body. I felt loved beyond anything I ever deserved. As I awoke from my dream, I knew I belonged to a loving King.

    The encouragement from this dream keeps growing inside my heart. The more I think about it, the more joy rises in me. When we *know* we belong to the King, that alone will keep our heads up no matter what the enemy throws at us. We are OWNED by God! Get that. What freedom there is in knowing that we are not our own, but The Lord's. He's got us. Be encouraged by this truth: You Belong.

It encourages me to know that Revival is on God's heart (it was highlighted to me in this dream—remember the scarf?). Though the enemy may harass us with troubles, God will prepare a table for us in the presence of our enemies. He has not forgotten us. He knows we need to be revived, and He knows precisely how to get it to us.

*Today, remember Who you belong to!*

**From Pitiful to Beautiful-Comforter**

I have noticed in relationships, including ones in my past, being emotionally "needy" leads to great disappointment, leading to depression. I don't know how the human heart becomes deficient in what it needs, other than not knowing God's Love and the Comfort of the Holy Spirit. Comfort is important. It brings peace and rest-something we all need in our life. I'm not talking about the comfort of a good mom, spouse, or friend. I'm talking about the comfort that only God can supply at a deeper level. His comfort soothes the soul.

I had become so emotionally needy, and I expected those around me to fulfill my emotional needs. They couldn't, but I expected them to. I put expectations on them they could not live up to. I expected others to make me happy and keep my life peaceful. That did not work. It only caused arguments that left me wounded. Others put these same expectations on me, too, and I couldn't do it. I could not maintain their peace. I couldn't make anyone happy. No matter how hard I tried.

This scenario reminds me of the bondage of the Hebrew children under Pharaoh's rule. God's people were slaves to the Egyptians for four hundred years. **(Exodus 1-12)** They were under terrible slavery that worked them to death. They were commanded to work more and more. Their load was more than they could bear. What they were asked to do was impossible to complete. They couldn't make it happen.

I was relating to these slaves (with significant differences, of course). I did not realize how hard I worked to make people happy and how guilty I felt when I couldn't. I could not make it happen. It was impossible. I felt like a failure. It left me insecure and afraid. I thought something was wrong with me. What a lie! It is not our responsibility to fulfill someone's life. We cannot maintain their peace or fill them with joy. We are not able to do that. The human heart belongs to God, even mine. Only God can fully satisfy.

At times, I was living like a master. Now that's confusing. I went back and forth from a master mentality to a slave mentality. I barked out demands and worked feverously to please. There was a constant struggle for control. I was needy and those I loved were needy, too. What a mess! We needed peace that only God can give.

    I found peace in the arms of God. I needed to know Him as the One who could love me perfectly. I needed to experience Him as the Comforter that cared for all my emotions. No one can comfort me or soothe me like God does. I had to learn to turn to God with everything I was feeling inside. I had to give Him my anger. Yes, I vented a time or two. I had to give Him my fear. I would tell Him when I was scared and asked Him for peace. I had to give Him my pain and my insecurities. I learned to go to my heavenly Father as a child climbs into the lap of a loving mother. I needed Him to comfort me. We all do.

    One night while lying in bed praying, I asked God to touch me with His peace. I needed Him to soothe and settled me. I was a jittering mess on the inside. I waited for Him to come to me while forcing myself to relax the best I could. I felt Him pour over me a warm sensation that started at my feet and then moved up my entire body. My heart became warm and still. I fell asleep calm, cozy, and warmed by His Spirit, the Comforter. All we have to do is ask.

*May the warmth of God's tender presence nurture our hearts to wellness. Only You, Lord, can touch the depths of our soul. Holy Spirit, we need you.*

**From Pitiful to Beautiful-Finding Treasure!**

I had a dream I was in a prison yard. There was a wooden privacy fence that closed me in. I was running to escape when two black guard dogs attacked me. These two dogs were not trying to bite me; they were trying to take my shoes. I fought against them, trying to keep my shoes on my feet because I needed them to run. I'm not sure who won the fight.

I found an opening in the fence and left the prison yard. I started up this mountain that had a rough and muddy road. I was going to a small house, a place I felt was safe. It was a small green shack. As I made it to the top, I stepped into the yard. I looked around and found myself standing beside a bunch of trash. I knew that it was mine. As I looked around, I saw bright red ripened strawberries in this pile of garbage. The more I looked the more luscious berries I found. I then woke up.

I knew The Lord was showing me I was bound (in the prison yard). I assumed the black guard dogs were the enemy trying to rob my peace as shoes can represent the gospel of peace. **(Ephesians 6:15)**. I was sure the road up the mountain was my journey to a safe place. I was clueless about what the strawberries in the heap of trash meant. I only knew that I had garbage in my life.

I pondered this and could not figure it out. I have heard people say strawberries could represent romance or one of the fruits of the spirit, but nothing resonated within my spirit. I prayed and waited for God to tell me. I wanted to know what the strawberries meant. I needed to know what was in the pile of trash. Surely, it was something good.

Days Later, while sitting on my front porch watching my children play, the presence of God moved in like a breeze. I could feel the ushering in of the anointing. Holy Spirit seemed to settle there with me. I asked again, "What do the strawberries mean?" And I heard, "tranquility." As I listened to His voice, I felt tranquility and peace within my spirit. I sensed a serene Presence around me and did not want it to go.

I share this to encourage you in "hope." We don't know what is in all our garbage, but God does. Often, we focus on all the problems, emotions, lack, etc. But there is something spectacular beneath it all. For me, in the rubbish of depression and panic attacks, The Lord was saying to me, "You have tranquility, Becky." It may have been buried beneath the garbage, but it was there.

***"In the house of the righteous there is much treasure." Proverbs 15:6a*** *Search out your treasure. Peace to you!*

**From Pitiful to Beautiful-Pursue Joy!**

My heart cries out for a mighty outpouring of the Holy Spirit! I cannot wait for *revival*! I believe revival is within our grasp, and I believe we must press on! When I think about it, I can feel it. Even now, as I write, the fire of God rises upon my head, and I have an awareness that it is coming! Until then, I hear the Lord saying, "Pursue Joy, chase it and run after it. For in My Presence is the Fullness of Joy!" **(Psalm 16:11).**

We must pursue His presence and His joy. It is easy to become heavy in our spirits and overwhelmed with anxiety and sorrow because of circumstances that arise. If we take a moment to pursue His joy, we will be strengthened and then we can strengthen others. **"…for the joy of The Lord is our strength." Nehemiah 8:10** We don't have to wait for it. We can get it! Allow yourself to laugh. Think upon funny memories and laugh about them.

Laugh out loud! Stir up the joy inside of you-crack (clean) jokes. Allow the fountain of many rivers to flow. Seek it for those you love.

Once I had a heavy burden for someone I truly loved. It seemed there was nothing I could do to help her in this situation. My heart was broken for her, and I wanted the circumstance to go away. I cried out to God and heard Him say, "Pursue joy." I sat down with Him and began looking up scriptures on joy. I wrote down several verses and prayed His Word over my loved one. My mind kept going back to the scripture, **"Your words were found, and I ate them, and Your word was the joy and rejoicing of my heart; for I am called by Your name." Jeremiah 15:16**

Joy is precisely what my loved one needed. She needed to hear God's Word and have a profound revelation and understanding that *joy* belonged to her! I prayed for her to find His Word. And you know what? When I saw her the very next day, I could see that my loved one had found the Joy of the Lord! She shared her story with me about something particular God showed her in His Word. I witnessed the joy in her tears and His presence beaming from her face. And you know what? Rejoicing rose in my heart too. The burden left me.

Pursue His joy! Let us begin by eating His Word. Ask the Lord to lead you in this pursuit as He did me. He will do it. Chase it, desire it, and be filled with joy!

*I pray you are filled to the fullest with His Joy! May His Word be illuminated to you, changing your heavy heart to a rejoicing heart!*

**From Pitiful to Beautiful-Listen to the Rain!**

    I remember an encounter with an angel several years ago. I was taking a nap on our couch. It was raining extremely hard outside which, made it an excellent day to take a nap. As I was sleeping, I woke up in the spirit to an angel standing by my head. She was talking to me. She (sounding like a woman) said, "Look at the sun Becky, look at the sun." She would gently turn my head toward the window. I could see the sun brightly shining outside. She repeatedly told me to "Look at the sun." I continued to position my head toward the sun as it was shining on my face.

    As I would feel the sun on my face, incredible joy and energy would move through me. I kept my face toward the sun soaking in this incredible encounter, which changed my life forever. The energy I felt seemed exciting, joyful, and powerful all at the same time. There were no words to explain what was happening in me, but I knew I never wanted it to end. As I kept my face toward the sun (Son), I heard Jesus say, "I will come again for you."

As He moved away from me, going back into the heavens, I groaned from the depths of my spirit. He moved farther and farther away. I cried and gasped for Him desperately, not wanting Him to leave me. I loved His presence. I wailed in such desperation, just wanting to be with Him. I love Him so.

When I woke up, I could hear it was still raining outside. I had never felt such energy like that before. I did not want it to end. It was the most beautiful feeling I ever felt. I can say that since that day, a lot of changes have taken place in my heart. I believe "hope" came to me that day at a new level. **"Looking for the blessed hope and glorious appearing of our great God and savior Jesus Christ" Titus 2:13** What a day that will be! "Rejoice because your name is written in heaven." **(Luke 10:20)** When times get hard, and we know they will be on occasion, set your heart on the *hope of heaven*. There is where your name is written, and He will return for you. What Joy!

There have been times I've shut down all other thoughts to force myself to think of the eternal. Heaven is real. Remembering to thank God for His Son and for saving my soul has lifted my hope to new heights. Our hope is only in Christ. We can only find pure joy in Him. Jesus said, **"That where I am there you may be also." John 14:3b.**

If you are working in another state or country, if you are home lying-in bed listening to the rain, you can say you are never alone. He is always with us. Wherever He is, wherever we are, He is with us now! Are we still talking about the eternal? Yes! Now, more than ever. We will be with Him in Heaven, and through Holy Spirit, we are with Him now.

*Enjoy the rainy days. The Son still shines on us. Request His presence and rejoice- for your name is written in heaven!*

**From Pitiful to Beautiful-Flickering Stars!**

**"You have ravished my heart, My sister, My spouse; You have ravished My heart with one look of your eyes, with one link of your necklace." Song of Solomon 4:9** I love the beauty of the night because The Lord has been faithful in meeting me there. As I pray while gazing into the night's sky, He makes me feel like the only woman in the world! In His Word, He says that we ravish His heart; however, it is *my* heart that feels ravished by Him.

I love being alone with the Lord. He floods my heart with such compassion and fire. His presence moves right through me, causing me to love Him more! I get overwhelmed with the thoughts of a Supernatural God caught by one look from my eyes. My nights are beautiful because they are His.

One night as I was gazing into the sky, I

noticed the brightness of the stars. I had been praying and was drawn to the night sky. I noticed one star flickered. As I continued watching it, I heard The Lord say, "No light of mine should flicker." I burst into tears because I knew He was talking about His bride. I repeatedly said to Him, "No Lord, none that is yours should flicker, none should struggle."

Compassion moved through my heart for God's people. Many faces and situations came flooding through my mind. I cried out to the heavens asking for help for His bride. Not especially for the people themselves, though I loved them and wanted to see healing in all capacities, but primarily because I love Jesus. I wanted Him to have the best and brightest stars of all! "Not one flickering," but burning bright in His most incredible beauty.

I pray that you would become an illumination of His light! May there be no lack in your life. I ask The Lord of the heavens to visit you tonight, to heal your body, mind, soul, and spirit at all levels. Oh, seek Him in the night! Gaze at the stars and let God's compassion and fire consume you!

*May the Glory of God be seen in your life as your spirit shines bright with His beauty! Tonight-be ravished in His love!*

**From Pitiful to Beautiful-Warring Soldiers**

One day, The Lord gave me a vision of a battle. In the vision, grenades were being thrown, and I could see smoke. I was aware of gunshots and exploding bombs. I sensed the vibrations from the earth. As I looked around me, I could see wounded soldiers on the ground. I watched as others were running for cover. I could almost smell the smoke. I felt like I was physically there. It was a raging, chaotic scene.

I thought, "Wow! Is that what warfare looks like?" Is this what a spiritual battle looks like? How do we get through it and help those who have fallen?" As the vision continued, I bowed my head. I stayed focused on the mission at hand and followed every command. I drug the fallen soldiers under a tree of safety. I believe the tree represented the covering of the Lord.

As I meditated on what I had seen, the Lord spoke to me a vital revelation every believer should know. *"You must see through the eyes of the Spirit that your battles are not with people but those things that have hit them and caused them to fall."* The bullets, bombs, and grenades were attacks from the enemy.

People fall into addiction. People get hit with a spirit of lying. Some people have extreme anger and jealousy, making themselves and others around them miserable. And how do I rescue them? Do I pass them by and say, "You made your bed now lay in it?" What about those captured by the enemy as "Prisoners of War" who have given themselves to the passing of judgment and gossip affecting everyone they know? Ouch!

I believe The Lord has shown us clearly how to win these battles. The scriptures are clear that we are not in battle with a person, but with those things that influences that person. We wrestle against principalities, darkness, and wickedness.
**(Ephesians 6:12)**

**Stand therefore, having girded your waist with truth, having put on the breastplate of righteousness, and having shod your feet with the preparation of the gospel of peace; above all, taking the shield of faith with which you will be able to quench all the fiery darts of the wicked one. And take the helmet of salvation, and the**

**sword of the Spirit, which is the word of God; praying always with all prayer and supplication in the Spirit, being watchful to this end with all perseverance and supplication for all the saints. (Ephesians 6:14-18)**

Now I see more clearly what the Lord is saying to us. As soldiers in battle, we should keep our head low in humility (Helmet of Salvation), stay focused following our Lord's every command (taking up the Shield of Faith) and bring those who have fallen to a safe place of covering (praying always with all prayer and supplication in the Spirit, being watchful to this end with all perseverance and supplication for all the saints). There's much more to this passage of scripture, of course. These are only a few things The Lord was speaking to me.

If we could see in the Spirit daily, we would see people being hit and tormented by the enemy. Would we leave them lay and listen to their screams? No. I believe we would fight for their rescue. My heart changed when the Lord revealed this to me. It increased my compassion, caused me to forgive, and changed my perspective. Offenses and bitterness flowed out of my heart that day. I now see who my real enemy is. I'm forever thankful.

Let me encourage you to fight well, keep yourself humble, and do not return evil with evil but follow Christ's example. Remain focused and obedient to Holy Spirit's guidance. He is our helper, and He will lead us to victory. **(John 14:16)** Never stop praying for those entangled by the enemy's ways. For our prayers are powerful weapons given to us. The Lord will answer!

*Father, I pray that every reader keeps the faith to fight to the finish. Anoint us to rescue the fallen soldiers and lead them back to you.*

**From Pitiful to Beautiful-Butterflies**

I was in an all-day Freedom Encounter event that teaches freedom in Christ. These meetings are designed with a time of worship and prayer to pursue Jesus and His cleansing. We gather to take communion, to pray, and to worship. Then faithfully, God moves through the house in healing and freedom! These meetings are very powerful.

During the lecture of one particular meeting, The Lord showed me a vision. I cannot recall what the leader was teaching, but I will never forget the vision. The Lord showed me a field of butterflies and they were flying toward the sun. The grass was rich green and tall, and the sun set in front of me at eye level. The sun was huge. The butterflies varied in shape and color. Some were plump, large, and healthy. Others were thin and very weak. Some had missing or broken legs and broken antennas. I noticed some of them had damaged wings or underdeveloped ones. It looked as though some even had mud on their face.

Most of the butterflies had white wings thickly trimmed in black, having light brushes of pastel colors. Some were brushed with yellow, pink, purple, and other soft colors. I recall seeing a few butterflies that were a light yellow thinly outlined in black. Some were flying alone, and some were flying in small family units. They were all headed to the sun.

I saw myself as a healthy, plump butterfly. I had a few brushes of light pink on my wings. I was healthy, and I felt strong as I flew toward the sun with the others. I looked over and saw a little butterfly right beside me. She was crying and struggling to fly. The wind was blowing against her, and I could see that she was having a hard time flying. I felt so sorry for her. She was worn out. She was just a little thing, trying her hardest to fly. Compassion overcame me; I knew I could not pass her by. So, I slowed down as I gently lifted her with my large wing that was strong enough to power through her storm. She was crying, and I knew she needed my help to get to the sun. I looked around at the others. My heart hurt because I knew some had fallen in the grass. The wind blew some over, and others were too weak and mangled to fly, so they fell. We all had one focus, and that was getting to the sun.

The sun was huge and bright. The scenery was beautiful, quite heavenly. I knew the sun was our destiny and our destination. It was larger than all of us combined, allowing plenty of room. There was no need to be in a hurry. The sun wasn't moving, just the butterflies. Then The Lord spoke to my heart, "COMPASSION. Have compassion for them all. Help those you can, not only the tiny ones or the sick ones, but also the seasoned ones. Everyone needs help." Wow, that broke me. Even the ones that should know how to fly need our help, and we need theirs too.

I cried over this vision for days. I knew these butterflies represented the body of Christ, the church, and I knew that Jesus was the sun. He is our destiny and our destination. I realized *I* needed more compassion. We can get too judgmental, too competitive, and too self-focused. I saw butterflies spiteful with each other. Some separated themselves from the rest. It was sad and was wrong.

We need deep compassion for one another, and I believe compassion will heal the division in God's people. It was great to see everyone flying toward Jesus, but as I looked closer, it was evident that the people did not realize their downfall. They lacked compassion. We all needed more.

There was plenty of room for everyone. There isn't a need to fight for your place. There isn't a reason to run off, leaving someone else in need. But no one was doing either. I am sure there are Christians full of compassion and helping the people, but I didn't see that in my vision. Jesus, we *need* You to help us.

*Jesus, I ask that you stop us in our tracks to fill us with your compassion. After all, You were moved with compassion and You healed **(Mark 14:14).***

**From Pitiful to Beautiful-Forgiven!**


As the Father touched my heart with His love, all I could do was lift my hands and cry, "I've loved so little but want to love so much!" Repeatedly, I cried this out to Him as He wrecked my heart. In that moment, I was overwhelmed with His loving kindness. I felt so clean and so loved in a matter of seconds. I wanted that feeling to stay with me forever, and I wanted to share it with the world!

Gazing at the stars, I pondered that moment of My Father's love. I could not help but recognize how clean and forgiven I felt in His presence. I was reminded of the woman in the Bible that washed Jesus' feet with her tears and dried them with her hair. Did she feel that way? Did she feel clean and loved? Jesus said, **"Therefore I say to you, her sins, which are many, are forgiven, for she loved much. But to who little is forgiven, the same loves little." Luke 7:47.**

In reading Luke 7:47, can we say that those who forgive much- love much? According to His Word, I believe that to be true. I believe that's our Father's heart. He has a heart so full of love that He forgives much! We learn in **John 3:16** that, **"God so loved the world that He gave His only begotten son that whosoever believes in Him would not perish but have everlasting life."** Our Father loved so much that He sent His Son to shed blood for the forgiveness of our sins. Love moved Him. Love sent Jesus to the cross to die. God loved us so deeply that He sent the ransom of shed blood so we could be His! How forgiving is that?!

Remember every sin from this moment (and all past sins) is washed clean when we become born again, under the blood and in covenant with God. Amen! It is as though no sin was committed if we surrender all we are completely to Him. How loving is that? The price was paid! What manner of love is this?! This is the love God "so loved the world" with.

*What can wash away my sin? Nothing but the blood of Jesus!*

**From Pitiful to Beautiful-God is Good!**

There was a time in my life I loved to smoked cigarettes. I thought there was nothing like a menthol cigarette and an ice-cold Mountain Dew. Lol! That seems like such a long time ago. I remember smoking cigarettes and reading my Bible while getting hammered in the Holy Ghost! I would set my cigarette down and then jump up and dance a jig while speaking in tongues all at the same time! I then sat back down and read a little more, just puffing away. No joke. It happened. Lol!

My goodness, those are some days to remember! I'm so grateful, so thankful, that God isn't religious; instead, He is good! Eventually, I prayed about quitting smoking, but I didn't want to. I was halfhearted. In the beginning, I prayed that I would have the desire to quit. After a while, I prayed to stop. It seems I prayed for about a year, and I clearly remember the day The Lord set me free.

I was at home in my kitchen. I had cooked dinner and was cleaning up the mess. Suddenly, The Spirit of God entered the room. I could feel His presence as though a cloud was hovering. I heard The Lord say, "When you die, you will go to heaven; but your destiny requires holiness." Well, I knew what He meant; I was a preacher. I had a call on my life, and I knew smoking could not be a part of it. I sobbed and sobbed in His presence. I tried to bargain with God by telling Him I would not smoke at church. I said I would only smoke at home and keep it hidden. I was desperately trying to get out of what He was speaking to me. I wanted my destiny, but I wanted to smoke, too. However, The Lord came to answer my prayers. He waited patiently and tenderly in my kitchen until I chose destiny. Thankfully, He is good!

After I decided to follow His plan for my life, it gave me the power I needed to break free. I repented. I knew The Lord called me into ministry, but I still needed to rid myself of a few things in my life. Smoking was only one of many things where I needed His deliverance. In all honesty, The Lord has never left me without help. He has shown His goodness to me time and time again.

I share this to say; it is good to remind ourselves of the things The Lord has brought us through. It keeps our faith stirred and hearts captured by His love. I find myself in dilemmas from time to time, as we all do, so I remind myself of God's goodness. Those close to me know I often say, "Hey, God has gotten me out of far worse than this; I am sure He will get me out of this too!"

***"Or do you despise the riches of His goodness, forbearance, and long suffering, not knowing that the goodness of God leads you to repentance?"*** ***Romans 2:4*** *God Bless you!*

## From Pitiful to Beautiful-Blessed Beyond the Curse!

While battling depression and anxiety, I learned about generational curses. I had heard of them, but I never considered the possibility. Honestly, I never thought much of it. The Lord himself opened my eyes to this during a time of prayer and intercession.

I was in my kitchen praying for my children. I walked around my table repeatedly in intercession; I was led by the Spirit to do that. I could feel God's presence with me as I walked around the table while He led me in prayer. Midstream, I suddenly felt compelled to change the direction I was walking. I wasn't sure why I felt it was necessary, but I did. I continued in prayer for quite some time, weeping before the Lord for my family's sake.

The Lord then revealed to me that He led me

in a direction that would break off generational curses. Not only in this time of prayer but in my life as well. I was walking one way but needed to turn and walk another. Wow! I never thought of that. Generational curses? I was beyond thankful that He revealed this to me.

I wanted desperately for the struggles to stop with me so my children would not suffer. God answered my prayers by showing me the importance of breaking generational curses. He led me in prayer that would turn this around in the Spirit. He then shared with me how to further walk this out. It would take prayer and action.

Repent! Change your direction! Change the way you think and act. Yield to the ways of God by allowing His Word to renew your mind. I had to make choices that aligned with His ways, not the ways of my family or the culture. Every choice I made would affect me and those around me, especially my children. I had to be careful and resist sadness the best I could. I had to resist fear and muster up courage, even if it was only a small amount. I had to choose a different path other than the one I had been walking. It wasn't easy, but I did the best I knew. My children have been spared a lot of things; not everything, but a lot. Thank you, Jesus!

I had to choose His ways instead of my ways. God helped me by enabling me. He led me so that I could overcome. He shed His blood so I could live Blessed instead of Cursed. Jesus made the way; I chose to follow Him. How will you walk?

***And all your children shall be taught of the Lord, and great shall be the peace of your children. (Isaiah 54:13)*** *May you and yours be blessed through a thousand generations*!

**From Pitiful to Beautiful-Embrace the Call!**

In a vision, The Lord was speaking to me about "Preaching the Gospel." He was reminding me of the scripture, "How precious are the feet of those who preach the gospel of peace, who bring glad tidings of good news." **(Romans 10:15)**. I could see The Lord's feet hanging on the cross. My heart broke thinking about the brutal beating and crucifixion of our Christ. I heard Him say, "Am I not worth the preaching of the gospel? Am I not worth it?" In tears, I said, "Yes, yes, you are worth it! You are worthy of the preaching of the gospel!"

I share this, hoping to encourage you to fulfill the call of God on your life. Everyone has a purpose. God has a perfect plan for us all. **"My frame was not hidden from You, When I was made in secret, *and* skillfully wrought in the lowest parts of the earth. Your eyes saw my substance, being yet unformed. And in Your**

**book they all were written, the days fashioned for me, When** *as yet there were* **none of them." Psalm 139:15-16** (*emphasis mine*)

You may be called to be a doctor, mother, mechanic, teacher, or preacher. Regardless of what the calling is, He gave it to you. I was ten, maybe twelve years old, when God called me to preach. I have a friend called to be a doctor around that same age. Neither of us has ever forgotten the encounter. Usually, that's how you know; you do not forget the encounter. If you have forgotten, take a moment and wait upon The Lord. Ask Him to cause you to remember a visitation or impression you had from Him. If you remember it, chances are you should pay close attention to it.

Go back to the prophetic words that have stayed hidden in your heart. Inquire of The Lord and say, "Yes, yes, you are worth it, Jesus! You are worth the call!" If you are unsure of your calling, search your heart and recognize the deep desire you have. God places desires in our hearts to lead us to destiny. I'm not talking about "wishful thinking." I'm talking about a "Holy Spirit Driven" passionate desire deep inside of you.

It's important to pay attention to our thoughts and emotions. Have you ever noticed the nagging thought "there must be something more?" Have you been frustrated in trying to "find yourself?" All you need is to find God, and then you will find the destiny He has for you.

The enemy threw me around for years with the thought, "I am a woman." This one thought stopped me from saying "yes". I didn't realize my "yes" is all God needed to lead me to my destiny. I sat down with The Lord, asking Him to help me. While looking at His crucified feet, He reminded me of the night He called me. The surge returned to me. He spoke His Word and led me to my "Yes." Jesus is worth it! I've never been the same.

*When it feels like your fire is dim or your passion is weak, ask yourself, "Is The Lord worth it?" When you are unsure, and the battle is raging, ask Him to settle it. Look at His cross and embrace the call!*

_____

_____

_____

_____

_____

*Prayers ~ Thoughts ~ Impressions*

_____

_____

_____

_____

_____

**From Pitiful to Beautiful-His Strength!**

While sitting on my porch swing one day, I suddenly saw The Lord sitting on the banister. He was dressed in a long, thin white robe, and He had a black Bible on His lap. I bowed my head and sobbed. I am thankful, and I am grateful that *The One* whom the *Scriptures* speak about visited me in that moment.

At a time of conflict within my soul, there He was in front of me, so real and present in such a trying hour. I have learned that seasons of difficulty are seasons of opportunity to experience The Lord. For that, I am thankful!

It has been in those private and personal times with The Lord that I received the strength to endure. Grace is released in His presence, and we become strengthened with His strength. **"Seek The Lord and His Strength; Seek His face evermore!" Psalm 105:4.**

You may not immediately recognize that The Lord has strengthened you, but you made it; you are still here. Your life is proof that He gave you what you needed. He's your strength. Stop focusing on the difficulty but change your focus to *The One* who has brought you this far. Let us celebrate Jesus and the work of His Spirit that is taking place inside of us. It may not seem like progressive work when it's hard, but His work is always right! He will work all things together for good to those who love Him **(Romans 8:28).**

Some are currently in a season that needs spiritual strength to overcome. It can be a busy season for some, maybe a fun season for others, but the reality is some are going through a tough season. Remember to focus on The Lord and get alone with Him. Turn your current season into an intimate season. Everything you need is found in Him.

*May you seek The Lord and find Him, receiving all you need!*

**From Pitiful to Beautiful-Heart be Still!**

Are you struggling? Press in and talk with The Lord. Wait for Jesus to enter the room; He will touch your spirit. Wait on Him to come and overshadow you with *His Presence*. That's how intimacy works, heart-to-heart, spirit-to-spirit. Invite Him to come and sit with you. Invite Him into your thoughts and emotions. Relax, open up to Jesus and let Him in. Feel the warmth of His Spirit run down your back, and the chill of His awe flow up your arms. Listen quietly, and soon you will hear, "heart be still."

Intimacy with The Lord should be natural. After all, for the Believer, He resides in our hearts. We are in an intimate, ongoing relationship with God. He is always in pursuit of us, and we should always be in pursuit of Him. That's how lovers are. We continually pursue one another. **"…Let Him kiss me with the kisses of His mouth, For your**

**love is better than wine. Because of your good ointments, Your name is ointment poured forth; therefore the virgins do love you. Draw me away!" Song of Solomon 1:1-4a** Sometimes, when we are overwhelmed, we forget to go to the place of intimacy with our King, but it is necessary.

Moments with Him will overcome discouragement, disappointment, heaviness, stress, or whatever the problem. He is the answer! The Lord is all- powerful, and nothing is too great for Him. He is the Healer. He is the *Lover of our soul*, and there is nothing greater than Him. He is everything beautiful that lies within our hearts.

As this book is near its end, get alone with God. Ask Him, "Are you in this room, Lord?" Then wait for His presence. As you feel Him (or see Him), ask for His touch. He knows what we need, and He will be for us more than we ever expected.

*May your heart be still!*

**From Pitiful to Beautiful-Deeper Still!**

    Through God's grace, I've learned to maneuver through some challenging times. I have not learned this by myself or succeeded on my own. In all honesty, it's been the complete opposite. I have learned to lean on Jesus. **"Trust in The Lord with all your heart, and lean not on your own understanding" Proverbs 3:5** Let me explain.

    From the place of intimacy, I've learned to listen and follow by leaning into God. There were times I found myself in spiritual warfare or a naturally challenging circumstance, and I found help. Intimacy is the key. My heart would search for Him, and I would not stop until I found Him! I would lean into the voice of the Holy Spirit, and I would listen to the instructions of God's angels. Yes, His angels. He sends His angels to minister to the saints. They are always present and sent by The Lord. **"Are they not all ministering spirits sent**

**forth to minister for those who will inherit salvation?" Hebrews 1:14.**

I cannot stress how important it is to go deep into intimacy with The Lord. It is a spiritual place of love and devotion. It's a place that convinces us that no matter what, no matter how hard, or no matter how large, our Bridegroom King will help us!

I do not believe God loves others more than He does me or that "maybe" He will help me. I believe He will walk into my bedroom in the darkest night and shine His light over my emotions, bringing me the most beautiful peace that exists. Why do I believe this? Because of the intimacy between us, I am convinced He loves me.

Although I do not enjoy the hard seasons, I know that they come. In the middle of those seasons, I have learned to say, "Deeper still. May I go deeper into your love, Lord? May I have the honor to know you more? Take me to the depths of your heart, for there is where I find my peace."

*May you find yourself saying, "deeper still."*

**From Pitiful to Beautiful-Gold Digger!**

**It's the Glory of God to conceal a matter and the Glory of Kings to search it out. Proverbs 25:2.** Don't ignore the things The Lord shows you, and I implore you not to take them lightly. Pay attention to your dreams. Go as far as asking for them. Pay attention to the impressions you have on your heart and in your thoughts. Ask the Lord to speak to you. Read His Word and when it jumps out at you, know that God is speaking to *you* at that very moment! Make it an intimate moment and lean into Him. Ask Him to guide you into His heart. Search Him out; you will not be disappointed.

The Lord has hidden treasure in every word He speaks. It is His glory to conceal these treasures, and it's our glory to search them out. When we discover the glory of God (in any situation), it is like finding precious jewels. Real treasure. And when we search for Him and Christ is revealed to our hearts through His precious Holy Spirit, *In Him* we have found pure gold! Jesus is the most *valuable* treasure of all.

    Gold, a gift the Wiseman brought to Jesus. Think about it. Could this be because Christ is the answer, and the world is waiting for Him? Yes. I believe so. He is the answer to healing. He is the answer to freedom. He is Salvation.

    I pray that you will search for Jesus by seeking intimacy with Him. Become a *Gold Digger*. Seek Him daily. Set your heart on your relationship with Him. As you discover The Lord as the answer to your every need, you will fall deeper in love with Him. I pray that you become fully healed in the freedom that He so freely gives. He loves you dearly.

*I pray that every chapter of this devotional has brought love, healing, and freedom in Christ. God Bless you.*

Jesus,

    I love you.

Becky Keener studied at Assemblies of God Appalachian District School of Ministry. She has been active in local church ministry since 2003 serving as an Elder, Women's Ministry Leader and Prayer Ministry Leader. Becky is currently New River Region's Prayer Coordinator for the West Virginia Prayer Alliance and is family to the Appalachia Prayer Center located in Jesse, WV. She is the face and visionary behind Mountain Momma Rising, a ministry committed to following Jesus into the harvest of Appalachia families. Becky is a conference speaker, preaches, teaches and leads and assists in prayer gatherings throughout the state of West Virginia.

Made in the USA
Monee, IL
08 April 2023